FADING ADS OF
NEW YORK CITY

FRANK JUMP

Foreword by Dr. Andrew Irving,
Introduction by Wm Stage, Epilogue by Kathleen Hulser

Charleston · London
THE
History
PRESS

Published by The History Press
Charleston, SC 29403
www.historypress.net

First published 2011

Cover design by Julie Scofield

Manufactured in the United States

ISBN 978.1.60949.438.4

Library of Congress Cataloging-in-Publication Data

Jump, Frank.
Fading ads of New York City / Frank Jump.
p. cm.
ISBN 978-1-60949-438-4
1. Advertising--New York (State)--New York--History. 2. Brick wall signs--New York (State)--New
York--History. 3. Street art--New York (State)--New York--History. I. Title.
HF5841.J86 2011
659.13'42--dc23
2011038134

This book is dedicated to Tucker and Eric Ashworth.

Both would have been instrumental in the making of this book and ecstatic about its completion.

Contents

Introduction

Frank Jump is a commercial archaeologist, plain and simple. There is no school, no curriculum for this discipline; one earns his degree by taking an abiding interest in the subject, be it Route 66 filling stations, vintage brick pavers or neon signs, and one delves into the matter. One gets involved. Frank's particular passion is one that I share as well: documenting fading advertisements on brick walls, visual whispers from the past found most commonly in the warehouse and factory districts and tucked away in the older neighborhoods of our cities.

Getting involved means canvassing these areas, locating the best examples of fades—Frank's sobriquet—deciphering their texts, often obscured or jumbled; perhaps researching some extinct brand of coffee, flour or stove polish; capturing these ads on camera; and, finally, presenting them in an accessible and hopefully enjoyable manner. I am happy to report that Frank Jump has done all this, exceeding expectations in every way. No one paid him to do this; he embarked on this ambitious undertaking without thought of compensation other than the joy that comes from a job well done.

In 1997, Frank Jump's Fading Ad Campaign began as a 35mm chrome photographic project documenting vintage commercial advertisements on brick faces of buildings in the New York City area. Some of these ads, he was delighted to learn, were more than a century old, touting all-purpose patent medicines, horseshoeing services, long-forgotten cigars and whiskeys. He began roaming the city, photographing them in earnest.

Obtaining good photographs is not as easy as one might think. One soon learns that walls are not to be photographed at just any time of day. Depending on which direction they face, sunrise or sunset may work best for bringing out that warm cast on the brick. For other ads that are faded to the point of near-illegibility—ghost signs—an overcast day may serve to best bring out the outlines of the letters. North-facing walls can be a bother, the sunlight never quite bending enough to fully illuminate the old ad painted there. Moreover, the conscientious documentarian is not content with shooting large ads on the sides of tall buildings from street level; he wants elevation to get the angle right. Frank has more than a few stories about talking his way into lofty apartments and businesses in order to get those shots that otherwise would be impossible. And, if pressed, he would also admit to scaling rickety fire escapes; stopping in the No Stopping zone of the interstate; and taking an unauthorized stroll on the elevated tracks of the J Train, between stations, snapping pictures, ignoring the conductor's commands to get the hell off. Had the MTA police arrested him for trespassing it would have been poetic indeed; all for the love of the sign.

Frank's pictures and experiences have been funneled into a website and blog, fadingad. com, an interactive and readily navigable format showcasing, as mentioned, the vintage wall signs of New York City and surrounding locales. And there are some pretty good ones, ones that will make you smile, ones that may have escaped our attention had it not been for Frank's intrepid odyssey that continues to this very day. Interestingly, certain signs found in Frank's pictorial survey have transcended media, attracting artists who render them as watercolor paintings. In these instances, the sign has come full circle: from being painted on a wall, originally, to being photographed to being painted and placed back on a wall. A gallery wall.

And so it was that Frank's Fading Ad Campaign would be recognized as something unique and valuable, the popular press, both here and abroad, running features about these hoary old signs and the man who captures them. Now that Frank has this book coming out, I must say that it is about time, for there is a fraternity of commercial archaeologists out there who anticipate turning its pages and drinking its contents like a parched pilgrim at a desert well. Frank once mentioned that of the thousands of ads he's photographed, many have already been covered up, vandalized or destroyed. Yet he took heart that many others "still silently cling to the walls of buildings, barely noticed by the rushing passersby." Well, this book will get people to notice.

Wm. Stage
St. Louis, July 2011
Author of *Ghost Signs: Brick Wall Signs in America*, 1989

On Advertising Legend Douglas Leigh

Although I had learned about and come to respect Frank Jump's work in documenting ghost signs, it wasn't until the summer of 1999 that I had the opportunity to meet him in person. Jump happened to be on a road trip, heading back to New York City, and took time to stop and see what I was doing as founder of the American Sign Museum here in Cincinnati. The museum was very much in its infancy then, and I had just begun to assemble a collection of vintage signs and sign-related items.

Several months later, I had the occasion to visit with Frank and his partner, Vincenzo, at their Brooklyn home. That opportunity was all about our mutual interests, and we've remained friends as both of our projects progressed. I will never forget that first visit to see Frank…

My trip to New York was a last-minute mission of mercy. The urgency had been created by a phone call I received from Ilaria Borghese, the great-granddaughter of Douglas Leigh, the creative genius behind Times Square's Great White Way. As she explained, Leigh's widow (and second wife), Elsie, was planning to clean out their former Upper East Side apartment in the next two days, and all was going in a dumpster. She said, "If you want anything, you'd better get up here and grab it."

I couldn't believe it—Douglas Leigh's incredible legacy being tossed in a dumpster. I booked the next flight I could get to LaGuardia. As I was scrambling to get details together, I remembered Frank's invitation from the summer before to stop by. I called him and, in a rather frantic voice, tried to explain my dilemma, asking if he could pick me up at the airport and let me stay overnight. "Sure," he said without hesitation. "You can tell me all about it when you get here."

He picked me up that evening, and over dinner, I rehashed my conversation with Ilaria and told him my plan was to get over to the apartment and save as much as I could. Frank said he would drive me over to the former Leigh penthouse first thing in the morning. He told me he had to be at work at noon that day but he'd do whatever he could to help up until he had to leave.

What Frank and I found when we exited the seventh-floor elevator was an expansive apartment with boxes piled everywhere. It was just like Ilaria said it would be: a bunch of workmen gathering up the boxes indiscriminately and loading them onto the same elevator for disposal in the dumpster waiting street-side. Frank and I were able to put the workmen off for a time while we scurried around taking stock of the various piles and trying to segment the archival items from the clothes, furniture and other personal items. Toward the end, we were actually grabbing boxes from the workmen's arms and stacking them to the side.

At one point, Elsie asked if we wanted "the Snowflake," and we both looked at each other and said in unison, "The Snowflake?" Unfortunately, I was not equipped to ship the several-ton illuminated snowflake that had hung over the intersection of 57th and Fifth Avenue every holiday season. By the end of the day, we were able to save a little more than seven hundred items, dominated by historic photographs, slides and sketches of Leigh's work and nearly three hundred cans of 16mm promotional films. We were even fortunate to save such things as Leigh's Rolodex and several personally annotated scrapbooks of newspaper and magazine clippings documenting Leigh's career.

When I founded the American Sign Museum, the mission was to inform and educate the general public, as well as businesses and special interest groups, about the history of the sign industry and its significant contribution to commerce and the American landscape. Frank Jump has played a part as preservationist in this mission, having spent the last two decades urgently documenting the history of mural advertisements throughout the five boroughs of New York City with his Fading Ad Campaign.

Tod Swormstedt
Founder of the American Sign Museum,[1] Cincinnati, Ohio
Former editor and publisher of *Signs of the Times Magazine*

Fading Ads

An Urban Archaeology of Life and Photography

This book tells two stories: that of New York City and its obsession with money, advertising and renewal over the last 150 years; and the story of the life of a teacher and photographer who has dedicated much of his time to documenting and archiving the hundreds of gigantic advertisements that were painted, often by hand, on the sides of walls and buildings. These advertisements mostly date from the late 1800s and early 1900s, but their traces can still occasionally be glimpsed today throughout different parts of the city. Many have disappeared; they either perished when the buildings they were painted on were knocked down or they were simply covered up by bigger, newer buildings going up as part of New York's ever-present desire to reinvent and rebuild itself. The destiny of other advertisements, however, was much less dramatic and more gradual. For regardless of the thickness of their paint or intensity of their original colours, their fate has been to s-l-o-w-l-y fade out of existence while exposed to the city's scorching summers and freezing winters, remaining open to the relentless cycles of sun, rain, snow and ice in a dense urban climate of pollution and humidity that inevitably takes its toll.

It is remarkable how many of these advertisements refused to succumb to the forces of time, fashion and urban planning and still remain visible from different vantage points around the city. From Carriages, Coupes and Hansoms in Chelsea (page 161) to Omega Oil in Harlem (pages 36–37), a good number of these enormous painted advertisements have endured through the years and continue to look down on New York's neighborhoods. Some are more than a century old and have graced the sides of the same bricks, walls and buildings since they were first painted. Others may have recently perished, but thanks to Frank H. Jump's intense interest and commitment to photographing and archiving these unique signs over the last fifteen years of his life, we are left with a rich historical record of this essential component of New York City's commercial and visual past.

Reckitt's Blue (page 12), for example, dates from about 1890, and Jump photographed it in 1997. The advert still survives today but can no longer be seen, as it was covered over by a new building in 2004. As such, Reckitt's Blue is an advertisement that connects radically different eras in the time it has stood there. When it was

Reckitt's Blue. Taken July 1998.

first painted, standing tall as an ultramarine blue attempt to entice the commuters walking by to purchase laundry whitener and keep their clothes bright and clean, the world was a completely different kind of place. For the most part, people did not travel at more than the speed of horse-drawn cart; electricity and running water were not yet established in people's homes; and the average life expectancy at birth was about forty-three. Medicine, as we know it, had not been developed; neither women nor black citizens were seen as being responsible enough to vote; and colonialism was still in the process of subjugating vast swathes of the world's population.

It is no exaggeration, therefore, to claim that the course of the advertisement's lifespan was not just as extraordinary in New York's history but also in the world's. For in the time that Reckitt's Blue has stood proud selling its wares to successive generations of New Yorkers, the world has undergone unprecedented and radical changes in its social, cultural and technological constitution. Indeed, the advert has witnessed the invention of the film camera, the automobile, the first airplanes, two world wars and the Great Depression, television, the jazz age, the jet engine, the rise and fall of Nazism and the Soviet Union, McCarthyism, JFK, the discovery of DNA, the Beatles, nuclear fusion, the civil rights movement, space travel, Picasso, the first men on the moon, punk and hip-hop, postmodern architecture, portable computers, the Internet, 9/11, the gentrification of New York and much else besides. Who would have thought a simple advertisement would endure the rise and fall of nations and ideologies, while New York and the world changed beyond recognition? Certainly not the men who painted it, whose livelihoods depended on their ability to make citizens look up and desire the goods on show to the extent that they became convinced that *their* lives would be better with *that* particular soap powder, *those* particular shoes, *these* particular tailor's shears.

Often painted up to fifty feet tall and twenty feet wide, in bold, attention-seeking colors designed to stir New York's citizens from their reverie and make them lift their eyes from the ground, some of the advertisements documented in this book were considered eyesores in their day. Mostly, they advertise products that can no longer be bought, made by companies that no longer exist, painted on buildings whose original occupants are forgotten, by men long

since departed. What remains are the faded traces of these men's manual labor, which was creatively marshaled into a form of advertising and rhetoric that was popular in its day, and which above all else used *color* to convey its message to the people walking below. And what *we* are left with, by way of the photographs contained in this book, is a rich historical testament to the city's past. It is a story told through images of a city that has seen many changes in character over the last two hundred years, not least the rapid shifts in fortune from commercial booms to near bankruptcy and a population increase from fewer than 50,000 citizens distributed across the five boroughs in 1790 to over 8 million today. However, the book is also the story of a man who has been present to much that life has to offer and has gone through a similar series of ups and downs over the course of his own lifetime, including having to negotiate the looming shadow of life and death from a young age, and who now teaches technology in a Brooklyn elementary school. A person who transcended this personal battle with life and death in order to document an important and vibrant part of the city's social, cultural and visual heritage.

I first got to know Frank H. Jump through the familiar lettering of Arial typeface during the late 1990s, by way of the e-mails that bounced back and forth between London, where I was based, and New York, where JuMp! lived. By 1999, I had gotten to know Frank Jump as a voice whose words were not just located on the other end of a telephone line but on the other side of the Atlantic, which had the curious effect of never being fully coordinated in time. Accordingly, the distinct ambience of a late-night conversation in London was met by a Frank Jump living in the full light of day in New York, his mind set to five hours earlier due to the time difference. Likewise, Frank Jump's late-night musings about the nature of life, art and photography at 3:00 a.m. were always placed in the incongruous context of watching the sun and defeated morning commuters pass by my apartment window. However, a few months later, on June 22, 1999, I was due to meet Frank in person for the first time at a conference and art exhibition at the HERE Gallery in SoHo, where he had some photographs on show. For once, we were coordinated in both time *and* space, which are, of course, the two most important themes of his photography.

In an e-mail I sent to introduce my thesis to JuMp!, I asked if he would be interested in discussing his work with me as part of a research project I was conducting in Europe, North America and Africa. The aim of the project was to document AIDS as a global phenomenon in terms of how people in different cultures experience, live with and understand the disease, particularly in relation to how experiences of HIV/AIDS affect the perception of time and existence; how different cultural beliefs affect people's experiences of the disease; and the limitations of language and the extent to which people's experiences, perceptions and emotions can be communicated or understood by others. I was particularly interested in the way art speaks to and is used to explore and understand these issues, not just in terms of how experiences of AIDS demand that the world is seen differently and how this manifests in art but also in tracing the trajectory of perception through art as the experience of living AIDS becomes normalized.

Underlying my research is a simple fact that is well known but often forgotten—namely, how the persistence of consciousness is associated with the body, the present and the passage of time. Obviously, time cannot be perceived directly, but nevertheless, there is an implicit recognition and heightened awareness in the way nature inscribes time—say in a flower, the changing seasons, someone's face, a building or the surfaces of the human body—that seem prevalent throughout your photographs and their subject matter. It seemed to me that JuMp! was working on many of these themes by way of a different medium, namely photography, and so I was hoping he would be interested in meeting up and discussing the issue of time and existence as it appears both in his work and life. I was particularly interested in understanding how perception of time, existence and one's environment is not just altered through living with AIDS, but how time and nature might resonate in different ways, perhaps, as part of a general reorientation away from death and back toward life. JuMp!'s photographs suggest that death is not the ultimate otherness after all but life (contrary to what some philosophers have implied), and in some photographs, this dialogue is made quite explicit, whether this is through their associations with memory and the body.

Time and space were also the subject matter of the PhD I was researching at the time. More specifically, I was undertaking a study about the perception of time and space as experienced through the framework of people close to death. The research attempted to understand how the world appeared to people confronting mortality, including the sometimes radical transformations in perceptions of time, space and existence that people undergo when living under such circumstances. These often extend into changes in self-identity, self-understanding and body image; in people's religious beliefs and commitments and concepts of the afterlife, nonexistence and eternity; changes in the type of imaginary worlds people inhabit in relation to their surroundings; changes in the character and meaning of nature and humanity; and of everyday social roles and interactions while entering a new existential territory or attempting to reclaim life.

I first e-mailed Frank after coming across his photographs of the enormous fading advertisements that adorned New York's skyline. His work spoke to me of many things, of the cityscape, of urban advertising and the scale, height and changing vitality of the metropolitan experience over the last hundred years. But most of all, his photographs spoke to me about time.

Attempts to understand the close and complicated relationship between time and human experience stretch far back in history, beyond St. Augustine (354–430), Epicurus (341–270 BC) and the pre-Socratic philosophers' early meditations on time, to ancient Greek mythology in the form of the titan Chronos. By legend, Chronos was said to live on the horizon at the farthest edges of the world and, as such, was a constant but elusive presence on the periphery of human awareness who by some accounts ended up eating his own children. The implication here seems straightforward: time is both a creative and destructive phenomenon that is necessary for birth, life and death but largely exists beyond the sphere of human influence and understanding. The world and its contents are brought into existence by time—including

human life and consciousness, which could not exist if they remained static—but ultimately, things born into the world are devoured by it. Simply put, without time there would be no sentience, no body, no life, no death and no social existence, at least not in a form that we could recognize, insofar as human beings are formed as persons and raised in time; they carry out their domestic and working lives in time; they think, move and act in time; experience moods, feelings and emotions in time.

Since its earliest origins as a word and concept, time has been understood in relation to an *other*. Thus, human time is contrasted with the time of gods, trees, other-persons, rocks, the planet, science, infinity, stasis, eternity and the universe. Often the time of one society or culture—be that local, national or historical—is defined and imagined in relation to other cultures and other places. New York, for example, is popularly seen as a fast city whose citizens are fleet of foot and mind and symbolizes progress and momentum, in contrast to the slow pace of life in the village, countryside or the past. Nevertheless, the most resonant of *others* remains the phenomenon of death, for human beings always exist in relation to death and people's understandings and experiences of time stand against the human organism's mortality and finitude. A long line of philosophers—including Heidegger, Levinas and Derrida—have each ventured that death is the ultimate otherness. But while disciplines such as philosophy, psychology and psychoanalysis gravitate toward a search for universal themes and arguments that are shared across humanity, sociologists and anthropologists have suggested that death is largely understood as existing in social and cultural forms that mediate its otherness. Consequently, anthropological conceptions of death are relational to the life of the social group and focus on the relationship between an individual and the wider society and how time and death are understood through social, cultural, religious and material forms, including art.

It goes without saying that time is present in all artworks, from being able to look at a painting and see the movement of the wrist, the sweep of the arm and physiology of the elbow in a painter's brushstrokes as he moves his brush over the canvas to the rhythm and tempo of jazz or the dramatic pauses and silences in one of Shakespeare's plays. Likewise, a photograph cannot exist outside of time any more than painting, music and film can. The long-standing, but erroneous, cliché of a photograph as freezing a moment in time is called into question not just by variations in shutter speed but, as is beautifully demonstrated in Frank Jump's photographs, by the temporal passage and fading colors of the once pristine advertisements he documents. The cognitive and physiological constraints of the human eye mean that we can only see an image through time. Our bifocal eyes placed on the front of the head take in a panorama of nearly 180 degrees that encompasses almost everything in front of the shoulders; however, less than 1/1000 of the visual field is actually in focus, while the vast majority remains vague and blurry. This is why our eyes are in constant motion, by way of saccadic movements that occur at an average rate of three times a second and ensure that dramatic variations in focus and acuity are not noticed. Consequently, when we look at a photograph, as when we look at a landscape or during our normal everyday encounters

with people and things, the eye constantly and involuntarily scans the world in front of it so as to present a picture to the retina.

In Frank Jump's illuminating and detailed photographs of New York's fading advertisements, there are at least three different registers of time at play. There is the time that is contained within the fading advertisements themselves: a kind of social and historical time that bears witness to the passing of fashions, commercial possibilities and successive years of weathering, which in some cases took place over the whole of the twentieth century. Then there is the time of the artist, that precise moment when Jump took the original photograph, the particular assemblage of light, weather and aesthetic judgment out of which the photograph emerged. As Roland Barthes writes in *Camera Lucida*, "Of all the objects in the world, why choose [why photograph] this object, this moment, rather than some other?" Lastly, there is the time of the viewer who is looking at it, as if through a corridor of time, in which he or she is not just witnessing the world in the moment JuMp! released the shutter but the history of New York that is contained in the advertisement's fading colors as seen from the present. Nowhere is this more present than in Jump's documentation of the seasons in his series of images of Eaglo Paints—an advertisement that is no longer there—in which the different modes of linear and cyclical time are simultaneously at work. At once inexorably moving forward, time also returns in the familiar forms and colors of spring, summer, autumn and winter, highlighting the persistent relationship between time, metaphysics and art. Here, metaphysics is not meant in the modern, sometimes spiritual, sense but in terms of its original meaning of that which exists beyond the physical, including the phenomenon of time. We cannot "see" time. We cannot touch, taste or hear time. We cannot carry it or weigh it. In that sense, time has no physical basis. But we can detect the traces of time in JuMp!'s art, in the way that his photographs attempt to represent time at work and provide us with a visual and material record of its effects and passage.

On the day I eventually got to meet JuMp!, the location was a church on West 4th Street where a one-day AIDS conference and art exhibition was being held. The theme concerned the air of optimism now that the future appeared to have opened up, thanks to the new antiretroviral drugs. The stated purpose was to ask *what next?* However, I was struck by the fact that no matter how hard people tried to think about the future, about what was next and about where life would take them, they kept returning to the past. *What on earth was the past all about?* everyone wondered in unison. The crowd swayed together, occasionally moved forward again in time, but then would fall back into a sense of shock when its members looked back to the past: to the pre-antiretroviral era of the 1980s and '90s when thousands of young men and women were gravely ill, dying or dead.

New York's nighttime descended on the city for Frank's generation in the early 1980s, when HIV/AIDS began to impinge upon the city. It not only exposed many thousands of people—gay and straight—to death but cut across the dominant cultural narrative of life as something that extends into old age. The strange discrepancy of young, healthy people succumbing in large numbers to disease and death in relation to an overall population getting steadily older reversed the seemingly established order of city life. By the early 1990s, AIDS patients took up 8.5 percent of all hospital beds. And by March 31, 2000, there were 72,207 known deaths from AIDS in New York out of 116,316 known people diagnosed, including almost 10,000 infants. Moreover, for every diagnosed person, numerous others are affected, including friends, partners, parents, children, neighbors, relatives, acquaintances, counselors, medical staff, volunteers and work colleagues. These persons are also "living with HIV/AIDS" insofar as their lives become intertwined with a complex and life-threatening disease, forming a polythetic population of infected and affected persons across New York that crosses sexualities, genders, generations and neighborhoods and composes a substantial proportion of the city's entire population.

Given such a history, it is unsurprising that the conference and exhibition contained a sense of trepidation about the present and betrayed a complex mixture of anxiety, uncertainty and hope about the future: *what next?* As I walked around the exhibition, I remember overhearing one guy who said that because he was from the South and his mama had brought him up to be polite, he was going to treat the disease as a guest. He said he was going to be the best host possible, make it comfortable in his body and look after it right until it was time for him or his guest to leave. The man he was talking with said he hated AIDS from the depth of his guts to the top of his head. He said he'd always hated it and always would, he hated having to acknowledge it, hated having to talk about it, hated taking medication and hated telling people he had the disease. As such, simply walking around the exhibition and capturing snippets of conversation was a highly revealing process—almost as revealing as anything in the artworks themselves—and provided a tangible sense of the diversity of responses, attitudes and ideas about HIV/AIDS. However, what made the atmosphere dense with emotion were the various stories, testimonies and life histories that were being spoken over the main microphone to the room. Some of these voiced descriptions of life with and affected by HIV/AIDS contained a casual abandon and some good jokes, while others were raw, angry and wrung out.

I had arranged to meet JuMp! after the conference on the church steps outside. Frank H. Jump, however, was early and had ventured inside; thus, the element of surprise was on his side. I heard someone call my name from somewhere out of the milling crowd. I heard the voice again, but I still couldn't locate the face. Then, out of nowhere came a face that declared itself "Frank Jump." Tall, handsome, wearing a set of pirate's earrings and an orange Hawaiian shirt came Frank Jump in person and extended his hand. As we shook hands, I caught sight of his Dick Tracey Special Edition Millennium watch. His early arrival caught me slightly off guard, and it took me a few seconds to regain my balance, by which time Frank Jump (assured and cool) was conspiratorially close and sharing his thoughts about art and life, a consequence of which meant an instant level of intimacy was demanded from myself. No cold formalism or stiff and stilted introductions here. We sat down to catch the last talk of the conference and then went out into the bright sunlight of Greenwich Village. Immediately to our left, a heavily bearded man stared. The man was surrounded by posters and declarations, wearing a sandwich board declaring that AIDS

was God's cure for faggots, and as we walked past, he shouted out that he was glad so many gays were dying of AIDS and would be going to hell. Do I remember being shocked?

Not by the sentiments, as they were a form of tabloid currency that was common enough through the late 1980s and early 1990s. But I remember I was surprised that somebody could be bothered to get out of bed and drag himself and all his sandwich boards down to such an event. After all, by 1999, AIDS had been part of popular consciousness for well over a decade and formed part of the everyday landscape of many major cities, including New York and, of course, the West Village. I remember looking into the heavily bearded man's eyes and finding them strangely docile, with a smattering of self-righteousness. I was curious more than anything, although no doubt he probably interpreted this as confrontational rather than curious. Frank H. Jump, meanwhile, carried on his conversation without a hint of acknowledgement. I kept meaning to find out the level of self-conscious performance involved or whether JuMP! had even noticed the man, his comments or his posters but never did; the conversation had moved elsewhere.

New York City is in large parts a municipality that was founded on trade and immigration, and as such, the city and its buildings and architecture testify to the complex, historical relationship among people, money, material goods, architecture and advertising. The city's vast surfaces provide a seemingly irresistible temptation to businesses and advertisers and provide a visible index of the products, fashions and moral standards of different eras. These somehow combine to form part of the content and character of the city we know today: diverse, contested and always in process, in the thrall of capital, often overly sentimental and, above all, full of nervous commercial and artistic energy. Indeed, like the human body, the nervous system of New York is never in the same state twice. It also ages and renews itself over time, betraying the effects not just of its past but its hopes and desires for the future. New York's surfaces, therefore, provide an ideal medium for inscribing advertising and other promises of life that the photographs in this book describe and document. Because many of the fading advertisements are more than a century old, they are often an attempt to sell goods, lifestyles and moral values that no longer exist and can no longer be bought. They remain weathered and betray the passing of the years on the sides of vast buildings, while the products that gave birth to them have been reclaimed by Chronos.

Taken together, the seventy-two or so fading ads presented in this book demonstrate how the surfaces of New York City combine to provide an ever-changing complexion that is made up of different hues and tones that change and offer a visible measure of time. Indeed, the close link between complexion and complex, which both come from the Latin *con* that denotes "with" or "together" and *plectare* (to plait or twine), suggests how the fading advertisements that make up such an integral part of the city's complexion can be read as the meeting point of life stories, urban dreams and hard-nosed and competitive attempts to sell aspirations and goods for profit. Although in modern usage "complexion" refers to the surfaces of the body, if we trace the term's meaning beyond a few hundred years, we see how complexion was also used to describe

the interior constitution and attributes of the person and their body or, in this case, the soul, content and character of New York City, a city founded on trading, traditions and artistic and entrepreneurial creativity, as well as corruption, decay, false promises and much else besides. If New York is a city in which prestige is dreamt about, worked for and occasionally wrestled from other people, it is telling that in its original incarnation the word "prestige" meant to achieve by illusion, delusion, trickery, deception, enchantment and glamour. Prestige and complexion: two of the dominant faces of New York that combined to create the social, cultural and economic circumstances for the production of advertisements on the size and scale of those that can barely be contained by JuMp!'s camera lenses. Here is the idea of the city as combining people's transient activities and ambitions with highly durable materials such as brick, stone, concrete and glass, in which working and consuming bodies live out their lives. It is not a new idea but one that stretches at least as far back as Aristotle's proclamation that "a city is composed of different men; similar people cannot bring a city into existence." However, when Aristotle made this statement, he was envisaging a city of nearer to ten thousand people rather than ten million, and so we are talking about a design for living that is qualitatively and not just quantitatively different. The modern-day city is frequently understood by sociologists and anthropologists as being modeled on the corporeal body—with the various constituent parts corresponding to different body parts and performing corresponding functions. If so, then the walls of buildings offer a layer of protective skin, practical in design and function but open to countless aesthetic and commercial possibilities and forms of advertising and decoration that have been enthusiastically taken up by businesses and good sellers.

The advertising possibilities presented by New York City's surfaces, which for more than a century have been painted by men in order to inscribe, ingrain and testify to the varieties and qualities of different products, were perhaps unequaled in any other part of the world. These advertisements are not just symbols in their own terms for a particular social group or generation of people but simultaneously condense cultural values and meanings that cannot always be articulated or put into language. Particular products may have helped define a sense of collective integrity, cultural identity and understanding and influenced people's economic choices and decisions within a certain neighborhood or generation. As such, they are also an index of class difference and inequality, whereby certain products are advertised in particular places to particular kinds of persons. Of course, given the demographic shifts and changes within the city, many of the fading advertisements documented by JuMp! don't tell us about New York City's neighborhoods as they are now but as they *were*. They contain within their paints the historical traces and demographic patterns of the city's population as it was rather than as it came to be. The paints accumulate dust, dirt and grime alongside rain, sunlight and the moral and aesthetic values of different generations over time, thereby creating a resonant and colorful epidermis that covers the city and can be studied to offer an understanding of the past. Even in New York City, bricks and buildings generally last longer than the generations that

occupy them, and seemingly old advertisements are encountered anew by each generation of new citizens, migrants and relocaters. As a generation dies or simply moves out to the suburbs, the dead skin peels off and is eventually sloughed away, only to reveal the advertisements anew to succeeding groups and generations. It is evocative of the difference between *cutis* and *pellis*, between the living skin that breathes and renews itself and the dead, discarded skin that has become scoured, loosened or simply fallen away from the body.

New York City, which until 1898 meant Manhattan and parts of the Bronx, was founded in 1626 and built on an island about 12.5 miles long and 2.5 miles across, covering only 22.2 square miles of contemporary New York City's 469 square miles. The city was built from south to north, with construction beginning at Manhattan's southern tip and expanding northward. By 1653, the city had only reached modern-day Wall Street, which marked the city's northernmost extension. By the first census in 1790, the population only consisted of 33,111 sometimes feverish souls; building had only just reached the modern-day city hall; Chelsea and Greenwich were outlying villages; Midtown was farmland; and large parts of the island were covered in thick woods, with many roads meandering in accordance with the population's agricultural needs. Ten years later, the population had doubled to 60,489. By the 1810 census, it had reached 96,373, and with a further massive, tenfold population increase anticipated over the coming century, the city councilors decided to "unite regularity and order with the Public convenience and benefit, and in particular to promote the health of the city," in a way that would contribute to the "free and abundant circulation of air" and help regulate odors and people. A major consequence of the potentially massive population increase was the city's current grid system, insofar as the newly formed city commission's first important act was to commission a plan for the future layout of the city. They engaged a surveyor, John Randel, to survey the entire island, with the purpose of transforming its woods, swamps and grasslands into a place "composed principally of the habitations of men, and that straight-sided and right-angled houses." Randel and his assistants spent the next three years painstakingly measuring and mapping Manhattan's entire topography, with a resulting 7.8- by 2.0-foot map, which offered unprecedented levels of detail about the island. Randel's map is even more interesting because it does not simply map Manhattan's topography, streets and buildings of the time but also imposes a design for the island's future, in that a grid system is laid over the land, determining where future streets would be built.

As often is the case, even the best made predictions, including the massive population increase of the city's commissioners, turned out to be wrong. The actual turn of events, scale and height of building far exceeded even their most extreme expectations, and the population grew from 96,373 persons on Manhattan Island at the time of Randel's map to 2,284,103 in the 1920 census. Thus, by the 1920s, a new sense of scale and structure had emerged, against which an individual born when farmland covered most of Manhattan could compare his agricultural practices and muddy, organic desires, especially after the invention of pressured water pipes and the elevator allowed for taller and taller buildings, simultaneously laid out on the logical principles and

Enlightenment rationality of the grid system of 1811. But while the city's commissioners may have imposed their will on all subsequent generations through their urban blueprint and its subsequent implementation in practice and architecture of their extended, straight avenues, they could not have anticipated the scale or verticality of the buildings. Instead, the rapidly shifting and feverish cityscape of New York provides both the impetus and background to the advertisements that became an integral part of the city and its history. A history that for the last fifteen years Frank Jump has attempted to document though his photographs and own unique brand of urban archaeology.

Today, the iron, brick, concrete, steel and glass materials of Manhattan's contemporary buildings combine with contemporary advertising and the painted adverts of the past to provide the dominant visible and aesthetic material of city life. The perspectival horizons formed by the city's buildings continually offer a series of extended surfaces and straight edges that enable New Yorkers to look far into the distance, much like a Euclidean drawing or one of Canaletto's paintings. A frame of receding perspectives and diminishing angles continually guides the eye toward a vanishing point on the horizon: a point distant in time and space, mathematically known in advance, subject to scientific reason, embedded in perspectival painting but lined by commercial advertising. It was during New York's most frenetic periods of change that the fading advertisements documented in this book were born and came into being, selling goods from the sides of buildings and the ever-increasing brick space of a city built not just along but upward. How curious it is that when citizens look up toward the sky it is not just buildings that look down upon them but huge, glaring advertisements selling products as diverse as hair cream and music. In modern New York at midday, 1.2 million people, a population greater than some nations, cram into the square mile of midtown Manhattan around the 34th Street area where many of these advertisements were, or are still, located. They provide something more permanent than the temporary patterns and ever-changing configurations of the crowded streets below, where the frenetic pace set by walkers at times can average up to 300.0 feet per minute along 22.5-foot-wide sidewalks.

Frank Jump still spends many of his evenings and weekends roaming around the city, looking for evidence of the passing of time. He still occasionally wears Hawaiian shirts and takes pictures of a whole array of persons and places. However, his main obsession remains documenting the fading advertisements painted on the sides of buildings. He captures them before they fade away and puts them on his website, and in this book, he has selected seventy-two among the many hundreds of slides to tell a story of New York as it is and as it was.

Frank was twenty-six when his illness was diagnosed, and he was told that he had "a couple of good years left." So he took himself out of the workforce and filled in all the offers for new credit cards and bank accounts that came to his door in the junk mail, thinking, "I've never got to pay any of this back." But Frank did not die. When we first met, he had been HIV-positive for thirteen years, had gone bankrupt and had reenrolled in college. Frank was acutely aware of himself as a body that

JuMp! in front of Eaglo Paints on Nostrand Avenue (pages 154–155) in 2001.

might disappear; a body in an urban landscape that, like the advertisements, was fading; a body that, like them, was not supposed to last long but somehow remained part of the city. Accordingly, Frank sees his reflection not in the mirror but in the fading colors of the advertisements that provide him with evidence of his existence.

Frank has mostly remained healthy, and HIV has been more a psychological burden and a brooding potentiality that overshadows his existence and calls his future into question. His body has responded to the disease in an extraordinary way, so much so that his body became an object of medical curiosity and doctors keep devising challenges for it.

In late 1999, some doctors wanted to know what would happen if they took him off his medications. Ordinarily, when someone stops taking antiretroviral medications, the disease returns stronger than before. This is one of the pitfalls of triple-combination medication. Once on it, you are on it for life—or you risk a more potent infection. You live with the side effects: distended belly, nausea, diarrhea, low testosterone, nightmares and the possibility of Crixivan (a protease inhibitor) crystals forming in your kidneys.

Frank agreed to stop his medications so his doctors could observe what would happen. They told him that he would become sick but that they wanted to know if the conventional wisdom was right—namely, that in chronic infection the body's ability to mount an immune response is lost forever—or if instead Frank's body would develop an immune response. After eight weeks Frank would resume his medications, and then the process would be repeated. Afterward, the amount of virus in Frank's blood would be measured to see if his body had fought back. Frank likes to throw himself into the fire, and this time he faced three bouts of miserable and painful illness. Because we kept in contact by e-mail, I already knew that Frank had volunteered to come off the combination therapy so the doctors could see how his body responded. Up went the viral load, down went the T-cell count and d-d-down went Frank Jump.

Frank e-mailed me:

My viral load has shot up from 0 to two million in less than 6 weeks. My T-cells have dropped to my lowest ever and I panicked. When I discovered these results I went back on antivirals (but only after I visited my physician who didn't check my viral load until my normal appt). The study apologized to me for not keeping me abreast of the T-cell numbers and let me know that my viral load was tremendously high. I said I'd try this twice more. If after the second time, the viral load increases as high again, I won't try it a third time. If the numbers peak at a considerably lower number, indicating some kind of "intelligence" on behalf of my immune system, I will try a third time. If this doesn't work—tant pis—I'm ready for another theory.

Now he's back and looks better than ever. In 2011, at the age of fifty-one, and exactly two hundred years after John Randel's map outlining his grid design for the city, Frank has been living with the disease for half of his life. He still hasn't documented every fading advertisement in New York.

Dr. Andrew Irving
Visual Anthropologist
University of Manchester, UK

Acknowledgements

With special thanks to my mother, Willy Jump, and my husband, Vincenzo Aiosa, for their unconditional love and support. Many thanks to Nelson Santos and Thomas Devaney for their insights; Amy Sadao, Jenny Ricketts, Lemmy Caution, Sandra Walker R.I., Kevin Walsh, Walter Grutchfield, Julian Seery Gude, Sam Roberts, Kathleen Hulser, Dr. Andrew Irving, Tod Swormstedt and Wm. Stage for their collaboration; and Lucy Winner, Mel Rosenthal, Joe Goldberg and Jim Greenberg for their guidance. For their generous contributions to the Fading Ad Campaign, I would like to thank the following people: Donn and Bob Middleton (Mack signs), Professor Mary Brabeck and Dr. Michael Brabeck,

Jay Lesiger and Tom Klebba, Frank Ligtvoet and Nanne Dekking, Andy Hughes, Isabel and Rosario Dawson, Sean Strub, Tama Starr (ArtKraft Strauss), Caroline Kim and Luis Santiago, Robert French, Raphael Carty, David E. Oppliger, Ronald J. Nigro, Neil Boxer, Patricia DeLeeuw, Kenneth J. Figueroa, Lindsay M. Wright, Brady R. Galan, Judith Ann Coffman, Phillip Brian Harper and Thomas Freedman, Jane K. Rushton, Samuel H. Havens, Kathleen Barnes, R.B. Caldwell and James Jaxxa, Elizabeth J. Misek, Lawrence Martin and Angela Martin-Fehr, Richard C. Richardson Jr. and Patricia B. Richardson, Margaret More Hunt, Apurva N. Shah and Chetna R. Shah, Malina Sahu, Saumil S. Doshi, Marion L.

Vetter, Budd M. Heyman and Mary Heyman, Patricia Hedieh Eshaghian, Sawsan K. Abdel-Razig, Celia Faye Stewart, Nathan H. Thompson and Robin Freeman. For their continued support, thank you to Betsy Gotbaum, Leslie Nolan, Barbara Snow, Jacqueline Girardi, Kevin Langley, Jon Nalley, Malaga Baldi, Bobby Rivers, David W. Dunlap, Nick Hirshon, Pete Anderson, James Lileks, Rory Albanese, James Duncan, Gaia Son and Bob Kovel, Eric Sawyer, Andy Humm and Terry Washington. With the warmest gratitude for sharing their family histories, I'd like to thank Beth Beeman, Aileen Schaefer, DeDe Burke and Michael Hughes.

New York City's Fading Ad Campaign

The Chrome Age

If I leave behind an act which I have accomplished, it becomes a thing by falling into the past. It is no longer anything but a stupid and opaque fact. In order to prevent this metamorphosis, I must ceaselessly return to it and justify it in the unity of the project in which I am engaged. Setting up the movement of my transcendence requires that I never let it uselessly fall back upon itself, that I prolong it indefinitely. Thus I can not genuinely desire an end today without desiring it through my whole existence, insofar as it is the future of this present moment and insofar as it is the surpassed past of days to come. To will is to engage myself to persevere in my will.
—Simone de Beauvoir, The Ethics of Ambiguity

Fading ads are a beacon in the navigation of an urban life. In the late twentieth century, the Fading Ad Campaign began as a 35mm chrome photographic project documenting vintage mural ads on buildings in New York City. Quickly, it became a metaphor for survival since, like myself, many of these ads had long outlived their expected life span. Although this campaign doesn't deal directly with HIV/AIDS, it is no accident that I chose to document such a transitory and evanescent subject. Of the thousands of ads I've photographed, many have faded out of existence, been covered over or destroyed. But still many silently cling to the walls of buildings, barely noticed by the rushing passersby.

In 1986, I found out I was HIV-positive. At age twenty-six, with experts giving me possibly four more years to live, I was immediately thrust into a midlife crisis and the curvature of space-time around me got more curved. Like a figure skater, I started to spin faster as I pulled my arms in toward my center, my speed increased until—I finally approached the speed of life.

Time passed so quickly that others around me seemed to grow old and die before my eyes. My urgency to leave my mark as a person and an artist who had walked this planet became intensified. I spent lots of money, none of it mine. I accessed all my available credit lines and bought a home recording studio. I wrote lyrics and music for underground theatre and film on the subjects of AIDS and homelessness. Much of the material was based on my experiences as an activist with the newly formed New York City–based group ACT UP (AIDS Coalition to Unleash Power) and my personal dealings living with this new, deadly virus.[2]

By 1990, long-term plans started to creep back into my consciousness after being banished by a dubious prognosis. By now I had met my lifetime companion, husband and collaborator, Vincenzo Aiosa, who played an active role in signs scouting for this campaign and later became a photo contributor for the Fading Ad Blog. In 1995, after almost a twenty-year hiatus, I returned to college to finish my bachelor of arts in music, theatre and film at Empire State College (SUNY), much of it based on my life experiences as a recording artist and activist. In February 1997, when I first discovered the vintage sign Omega Oil in Harlem, I had an artistic epiphany, realizing this was to be my next documentary photo project. What was not evident was to what extent this undertaking would alter my life's trajectory.

In November 1997, I agreed to exhibit this work in a public art space at the Gershwin Hotel for the annual Visual AIDS Day Without Art event as an "HIV+ artist." While politicizing my HIV status for the public good wasn't a problem for me, the project still seemed one of historical documentation devoid of personal experience and expression: the focus was the signs and not my life condition framing it. And even if I personified each sign and ensured to photograph its best side—like an aging diva that was once greatly admired—these images were primarily windows to our commercial and industrial past. They represent a time in American history that was filled with enterprising ideas and burgeoning global marketing, and I couldn't see how they

would fit in the context of an "AIDS art show" alongside talented artists whose work clearly and provocatively portrayed their struggles with the virus. It wasn't until my degree program mentor, Lucy Winner at Empire State, said, "Frank, there's a connection between your survival, the survival of these signs and your fervent passion to photograph them," that it all clicked.

Dr. Andrew Irving, professor of visual anthropology at Manchester University, describes how HIV/AIDS often transforms people's perceptions of time, existence and the body. Visual artists with HIV/AIDS often experience an accelerated life and reflect this acceleration of time in their work. Many of the artists I've known who are categorized as HIV-positive artists or AIDS artists, either by self-proclamation or by their audience, often express their experience with accelerated time in profound and daring ways.

Subsequently, I found a home in the Visual AIDS archive of past and present artists with HIV, whose works are displayed on the Estate Project website[3] in conjunction with the Museum of Modern Art. Thanks to this site, I became aware of a vast body of work to which I would otherwise never have been exposed. Today, I'm grateful to be included and associated with such a collection of talented visual artists and their brave expressions of personal struggle, including the challenge of making art in the face of mortality and finite time. Together they document a major historical event of the last century—the age of HIV/AIDS.

The sense of urgency I felt every day drove me to document New York's fading advertisements and capture the marks left by artists and artisans, most long since dead, who spent their lives painting huge commercial murals over the last 150 years. Some signs are over 100 years old and were never expected to survive this length of time. Like my own body, they weren't meant to last this long, and as such, there is a direct correlation between the signs and my own life experience and subsequent attempt to document their presence through photography. After accumulating an abundance of vintage ad images across America, I realized I was now committed to this campaign through thick and thin, health and sickness, for the rest of my life and was determined never to let my archive "uselessly fall back upon itself."

Within the last century, we have witnessed the constant rise and fall of countless businesses. Some manufactured popular products that are still being produced today, while others ceased production and only remain as a name on the side of a building, slowly fading in the sun. Many of the vintage ads I have documented were preserved because buildings were built next to them that covered them over and protected them from the elements. They remained hidden from the eye for decades at a time, only to be revealed again many years later when an adjacent building was torn down. Other images survived through the sheer luck of having a northern exposure—away from the intensity of the sun.

The images in this book provide a visual archaeology that reminds us of a bygone era in advertising and illustrates the past lifestyles, commercial tastes and social trends of New York City (and by extension much of America and other cities around the world) that use the sides of brick buildings to advertise goods and services. The images also speak to current advertising strategies and provide a priceless historical context for understanding the rise of commerce, socioeconomic trends and the demographic shifts and displacements caused by these economic and social overreactions in

New York, such as the white flight of the late 1950s and early 1960s to the suburbs. As such, the importance of these huge graphic landmarks must be recognized in the ongoing effort to foster interest toward their preservation.

Within a couple of years of conceiving and publicizing this campaign, I was asked to give public testimony in support of newer advertising before the New York City Landmarks Preservation Committee, where I compared historic ads with today's ads. I spoke on how preservation projects have the potential to establish a productive dialogue between ad agencies, local artists, local historical societies and preservation groups. Such collaborative efforts have since produced new site-specific, culturally sensitive advertisements in historic districts, for example, the work of Colossal Media in SoHo and Williamsburg, Brooklyn.

Embarking on the campaign has taken me to many places and opened up many wonderful dialogues with people around the world. On July 9, 1998, the *New York Times* followed up my exhibit at the New-York Historical Society with a front-page spread in the "Metro" section that brought widespread attention to the historical significance and contemporary importance of preserving fading advertisements. After the show came down, I decided to create a permanent home for this collection of images that would allow the advertisements to reach a much wider, even global, audience. So I launched the Fading Ad Campaign website in February 1999. The site has subsequently been featured in many online and print media, including: Archaeology Online,[4] POZ Magazine Online,[5] *USA Today*,[6] Yahoo, Forbes,[7] the *Chicago Sun Times*, the *London Guardian/ Observer Magazine*[8] and several radio and TV spots with the BBC, Canadian TV, Brooklyn

Original Fortunoff's store sign
on Pennsylvania Avenue near
Livonia Avenue. Painted by
Albert (Israel) Adelson for
Concord Co. (a family business)
in the 1950s

Independent Television,[9] *Leonard Lopate Show*
(NPR) and *City Arts* (PBS).

The campaign has afforded me a much
wider audience and has facilitated an incredible
network of correspondence with other fading
ad enthusiasts and historians like Kevin Walsh
(*Forgotten New York*),[10] Walter Grutchfield (*14th to
42nd Street*)[11] and Sam Roberts (*UK Brickads*).[12]
These correspondences and links to other
related sites have opened up a whole new
perspective of "lost America" and made me
aware of the growing interest in historical ad
images in urban and roadside environments. It
has also led me to some incredibly supportive
people around the globe who have become
lifelong friends and colleagues. Sharing the
campaign with our global community has
been exciting and humbling. It is like putting
a message into a bottle and tossing it out on
a sea of electrons. It seems so vast, yet it feels

like home. I'm always astounded when I try
to fathom humanity reaching out across the
vast electronic ocean of the Internet in search
of one another, finding like minds, finding
one's self and sometimes finding beauty. Never
before have we been so isolated from nature
and desensitized to violence and callousness
as in our urban environment, yet we still
are searching for connections to a greater
population, a global voice.

Today, we can look at a vintage Reckitt's
Blue or Omega Oil mural advertisement and
feel transported. Back when they were freshly
painted, some people regarded them as eyesores.
A century ago, there was a public outcry in New
York City against the proliferation of billboard
advertising, not unlike today's acrimonious
battle against the new "Times Square–style" ad
campaigns along Sixth Avenue, Houston Street
bordering SoHo and in lower Manhattan. I

do not think it is a question of whether or not we should continue to surround ourselves with larger-than-life images whose sole purpose is to move us to consume. It is a question of what images we may find enduring or possibly want to endure. When Joseph Berger of the *New York Times* interviewed Kathleen Hulser, public historian at the New-York Historical Society, she observed how "they [ads] evoke the exuberant period of American capitalism. Consumer cultures were really getting going and there weren't many rules yet, no landmarks preservation commission or organized community saying: 'Isn't this awful? There's a picture of a man chewing tobacco on the corner of my street.'"[13] Berger adds, "While a century ago, preservation groups viewed the signs as vulgar interlopers, some now want to sustain them."

Nonetheless, today's gargantuan temporary vinyl backdrops are disposable and very portable in comparison to the painted advertisements of other eras. Images printed in digitally pointillist perfection onto sheer canvases stretch across building faces the size of football fields. Some cover and protect older painted signs. A walk up Sixth Avenue from West 23rd Street to 34th Street is like a stroll through the land of the giants; overwhelming at times, it can also be comforting to feel like an insignificant grain of sand.

Advertising is and has always been the realm of the modern artist. When your canvas is the entire side of a building in a landmark neighborhood, there is a giant opportunity to be creative. If your target neighborhood is Chelsea, an area now known for its art galleries, trendy retail shops and restaurants, why not draw attention to its placement and make a bold artistic statement? There are some painted sign companies that meet this challenge to produce images that are not only enduring

but also provocative and at the same time classy, as in some liquor ads that walk the thin line between poking fun at the art world and homage. Some new ads even copy the styles of vintage ads and classical art (*Colossal Media*).

AH...NOSTALGIA!

In 1966, Pier Paolo Pasolini said, "If you know that I am an unbeliever, then you know me better than I do myself. I may be an unbeliever but I am an unbeliever who has a nostalgia for a belief."[14] The allure of past expressions in ads runs deeper than nostalgia. It is a belief that clutching onto the familiar as we plunge into the new millennium may inform our future decisions. These ads are something we can physically touch. They are markers of the passing of time. The rate at which technology is growing elicits new forms of social development. These signs are part of us and remain closer to us in terms of time and body than our grasp of what may come along. The Internet can either augment or attenuate the impact of advertising and human society depending on how much more or less prominent electronic advertising becomes on the Internet.

What other forms will advertising take in the next century? Will ads be even more temporary? Will they impact the environment in monumental ways, or will they become increasingly tenuous and miniscule? Will they be projected, holographic, canyon-sized images that disappear with the flick of a switch? Will they continue to beckon us toward the things we need; the things we don't have; or the things we can't do without? And will we ever again believe words like "the purest and the best"?

Gloria Steinem said on HBO's *Real Time with Bill Maher*, "Nostalgia is a form of obstructionism."[15] It is a moot point where we can move forward without looking back. Some individuals, communities and nations seem to progress with relative ease without looking where they've been. Others maintain the past as an ongoing reference to the present. Nonetheless, as the old forms surely fade, the new and upcoming ways of being call for new forms of adaptation. The challenge is keeping oneself ahead of the learning curve.

Recently, Professor Gerald Torres of Texas University in Austin said, "Nostalgia is corrosive and you need to banish nostalgia in my view,"[16] leading us to ask why Torres might say such a thing about the "good old days." Nostalgia is a response to the loss of discernible landmarks, within either one's external or internal landscapes. The loss of a familiar building or even a city block can be as devastating to an individual as a subdural hematoma. Our ability to effectively navigate our internal schemas underpins our sense of well-being and usefulness and to a large part is coupled with our ability to effectively navigate through an urban space-time. What makes nostalgia corrosive is if one soaks in it too long, it will dissolve our determination to recognize and give significance to those new landmarks that foster growth and equilibrium toward future proprio-coherent senses of well-being. Often we are anchored to our past through recollections of a younger, more vital self, which creates a dissonance when we confront our current self. Perhaps it is wise to banish this cause of stagnation—the corrosive eating away at our tenacity to move forward in life—which is an obstruction, often manifested in anxieties over becoming outmoded. Art

Gloria Steinem on HBO's *Real Time with Bill Maher* (Episode 82, September 15, 2006). Jump photographed the screen with closed captioning on. *Courtesy of HBO, Inc.*

forms and the media on which they are recorded are also becoming outmoded. Is the art of the "wall dog" quickly drifting toward obsolescence as well?

Jerry "Orange" Johnson, originally from Cleveland, Ohio, worked as a wall dog—an ad sign painter—for Seaboard Outdoor before establishing Orange Outdoor Advertising, Brooklyn's premier hand-painted sign company, in 1977. Johnson is perhaps better known for his "spoof" advertising murals, often depicting nonexistent products with classic nostalgic images accompanied by sublime ironical text. The following sign caught the eye of filmmakers for a documentary segment on PBS called *City Arts*, on which the campaign was also featured. Agility Nut writes about Johnson's *Penmanship Stupid* ad[17] on a personal website about roadside ephemera. The ad depicts Zsa Zsa Gabor as a pen manufacturing company representative:

> The Penmanship sign was located in Boerum Hill and was painted in 1997. It was a faux billboard created by Jerry Johnson of Orange Outdoor Advertising. Johnson painted satiric, retro-style paintings on this wall annually for about 15 years. Previous signs poked fun at subjects including: oleo margarine, electric companies, the Williamsburgh Savings Bank, plates, the power of cash and Ebbets Field. Sadly, this "ad" was painted over in 2003 (with red paint) and probably marks the end of the series.[18]

Over the years, several journalism students from Columbia University have contacted me about the wall dogs and the photo-documentation of the art of this dying breed of sign painters. One such student, Leila Abboud, in an article written in 2005 entitled "The Wall Dogs' Last Stand: Technology Puts Sign Painters Out of Work," focused on the quandary of older sign painters in a changing industry. Wall dog Alberto Gonzalez practiced his craft of outdoor sign painting on brick walls and billboards all over New York City for decades, balanced on two-foot-wide scaffolds that were hundreds of feet in the air and "braving the blazing sun, wind and cold to paint advertisements," only to face becoming superseded by a newer and cheaper process. Abboud further stated:

> The advent of digitally printed vinyl ads over the past decade has rendered painted ads nearly obsolete. Vinyl ads are cheaper and faster to produce, and neon and electric ads have spread. The union to which Gonzalez belongs once had hundreds of members. Now

there are a dozen. Similar shrinkage has occurred across the nation.

> With the sign painters will disappear the last traces of an era of American advertising when itinerant sign painters ruled. Nicknamed "wall dogs," these men traveled the country from the 1920s to the 1950s spreading the first national advertising campaigns. They emblazoned the sides of barns with logos for products like Mail Pouch Tobacco and Coca-Cola. The men earned a reputation for being wild, said St. Louis–based photographer William Stage, who published a book about the "wall dogs" and their work. "They would drink beer as they hung from rope scaffolds high above the street, and spill paint on cars and people below," said Stage.

> In many cities, including New York, traces of the wall dogs' handiwork can still be seen. The lead-based paint of the old ads survived time and weather. Although Gonzalez may think his craft is nearly extinct, his work and that of other "wall dogs" may not be forgotten. A small but devoted band of photographers and urban archeologists across the country has tried to preserve and document the remaining ghost signs.

> And in Los Angeles, outdoor advertising companies have seen an increased demand for painted signs after the city outlawed large vinyl draped signs two months ago. In Fort Dodge, Iowa, a building was torn down revealing a red, white and blue Coca-Cola ad on the adjacent building. The town is debating whether to restore the sign.

> "People are drawn to them because it reminds them of another time," said Frank Jump, a New York–based documentary photographer who has photographed thousands of old ads over the past five years.

Restoring old ads for historic or nostalgic value has become something of a trend in the Midwest, said Jump. [19]

When traveling throughout the United States, you will often see these fading relics "restored" by local preservationists and arts organizations. Personally, I feel these ads should be left alone to fade into imperceptibility, which is part of their natural life cycle. Although I understand the motivation behind re-creating these images to remind us of their former glory, for me, the fading quality of these images is a beautiful process to behold. Although I do not want to stand in the way of progress when newer signs cover these relics, I prefer to see them untouched. They've survived this long; they deserve to be left undisturbed.

Accordingly, the aim of this book is to present a photographic archive of some of the vintage mural advertisements I photographed during the first four years of the campaign in the five boroughs of New York City, with each image serving as a window to our past. Ironically, *Fading Ads of New York City* is in itself a documentation of obsolescence, for not only have many of the products these adverts touted as "newest" or "the best" become obsolete, but the medium through which I documented them has become obsolete as well. Kodachrome was my first love for the way that chrome slides produce a luxurious color representation of the world. The 35mm negative of the image is actually a "positive." The "positive to positive" reproduction was called the Cibachrome or Ilfochrome print—a high-contrast and rich color photograph that uses azo dyes on a polyester medium that does not fade. It was the preferred medium of artists, collectors and museums. Unfortunately, with the advent of

digital photography and output, this nonpareil process has become discontinued.

Inspired by the philosophy of Simone de Beauvoir, I cannot let this archive "become just a thing." It must move forward. I am committed to expressing the challenge and experience of living with HIV/AIDS in relation to the images of the campaign. These enduring images represent a surviving culture, shellshocked by famine and depression; world wars, struggle and emancipation; rhetorical scourges and over-the-top ad campaigns. They are living proof that we are even surviving capitalism, if only by the skin of our teeth. It is almost as if the human race was told we only have a few good years left to live. We are all living like it is the last days—strangely anticipatory and post-apocalyptic. Fortunately, I've gained a lasting view of my life and the life of this campaign, from more than just the sheer luck of a northern exposure.

Amateur archeologists can still unearth them, faded and weathered as they are, by walking the streets of the five boroughs.
—Joe Berger, New York Times

A series of twenty-four images hung in the corridors of the New-York Historical Society (NYHS) from August through November 1998 and can be seen on the Fading Ad Campaign website. How they got there is quite fortuitous. Just a year earlier, these images were captured on 35mm chrome. My photography professor at SUNY–Empire State College, Mel Rosenthal, always told us that as photographers, you should shoot what's familiar. Start at home in your neighborhood; start with what you know. So off I went to document "The Rise & Fall or The Fall & Rise of New York City" for our final project. Having grown up in

New York, the city was a neighborhood that I thought I knew well. But I never dreamed I would discover a hidden world that existed in silent decay. Rosenthal also said, "Pound the pavement to try to get a show." So I did.

At the Museum of the City of New York on Fifth Avenue on the northeastern corner of Central Park's Museum Mile, a lovely woman named Leslie Nolan told me that these images were worthy of a show but they didn't have time in their schedule for one. Nolan recommended that I go to the New-York Historical Society on the opposite side of Central Park, just a block south of the American Museum of Natural History. Nolan said the executive director, Betsy Gotbaum, was very receptive to exhibiting new documentations of "the city." Dale Neighbors, who was in charge of exhibitions at the New-York Historical Society, almost immediately responded, "Sure, we can exhibit these images this summer into the fall. I know exactly where we can hang them. How about twenty-four images?" My jaw dropped.

When I returned to class and told Rosenthal that I would have a show at NYHS, he demanded, "Get it in writing!" So I did. I faxed the press release to the *New York Times*, and the rest is history. When I saw Rosenthal again, the front page of the *Times* hung proudly on his office's front door, and he greeted me with a "you son-of-a-bitch" and a giant bear hug and a kiss. I am forever grateful for Rosenthal's guidance as a young emerging artist.

Much of what I learned about these images, the companies that were being advertised, their products and the sign companies that painted them was from standing behind people who came to the museum to see the show. I often went and listened intently. I went to the NYHS on many occasions that summer as a "fly on

the wall," just to see my work discussed by the crowd. What I thought was a minor exhibit ended up getting major press attention that led to me making connections with fellow fading ad enthusiasts around the world.

For the sake of organization and narrative, the original twenty-four images have been integrated into this book's collection by categories that are arranged to tell the story of the human body and how it moves through the city of New York's size and scale: forever propelled by desires and needs, we only need to look up to see how the story of the body is made explicit through the vast amounts of visible advertising on the city's surfaces. Indeed, it has become apparent that one of the major themes of this book is the relationship between people's bodies, advertising and the New York urban landscape over the past century.

The questions and challenges presented by the human body are a narrative that is writ large and continually played out on the surfaces of New York's buildings and walls. By focusing on such signs, we are offered a glimpse into the cultural, moral and medical values of past eras. Our bodies break down, a human failure that warrants cures and preventative medicine. Our bodies have needs that sometimes get us in trouble, either by the results of excesses or the consequences of social and religious constricts. Our bodies need comfort, shelter and security. Our bodies need pleasure and sensual stimulation. Our actions to fulfill these needs also pit our bodies against conventional, social and religious mores. Ultimately, our tired bodies decay and die. All the trials, tribulations, joys and pain of the body can be mirrored in these ubiquitous signs that envelop us.

Frank H. Jump

Omega
Oil
For
Sun Burn
For
Weak Backs
Omega
Oil
For
Athletes
Trial
Bottle
10c
FANTASY
ISLAND

Snake Oils,
Elixirs,
Tonics,
Cure-alls
and
Laxatives

OMEGA OIL

For Sun Burn, For Weak Backs, For Stiff Joints, For Sore Muscles, For Athletes. Trial Bottle 10¢.

Marketed as an all-purpose miracle oil, the company was incorporated from February 3, 1870, through April 2, 1924. Snake oil in American vernacular has a negative connotation that suggests medical quackery and hoax cures. In China, snake oil is used to treat rheumatoid arthritis and is proven to contain high concentrations of eicosapentaenoic acid or EPA, one of the omega-3 fatty acids.[20] Although the actual compounds in snake oil may have an analgesic effect, it has generally come to mean a panacea. An elixir—derived from the Arabic word *al-iksir*, meaning "effective recipe"[21]— is usually made with alcohol, not unlike a tincture that contains one particular active ingredient dissolved in alcohol, and is usually pleasant tasting. Again, the use of elixirs suggests miraculous cures and panacea. Many liniments were highly aromatic and contained salicylic acid (aspirin) and capsaicin (active ingredient in hot chili pepper). All of these purported medicinal products were marketed and sold during the turn of the twentieth century all over the country, and perhaps first in New York City. One just has to begin a journey on an urban yellow brick road in a spiral search of one of these ancient hucksters, and he will soon hear their tireless and faded siren's song beckoning to him.

The giant wall mural of Omega Oil is one Emerald City example of the guaranteed claim to remove your pain and cure your ills. Today's equivalent would be television commercials promising to remedy erectile dysfunction, baldness or depression. "Ask your doctor about…" I'm sure physicians just love their patients coming in with self-diagnosed and self-prescribed ailments they are sure they possess. At least one hundred years ago, you could have gone to the chemist or druggist and said, "Give me a bottle of Sloan's Liniment. Got a bad flare-up of the rheumatiz." Perhaps the trusted balm would work. We have more control over our illnesses than we fully comprehend. Today, people walk into their physician's office with a litany of self-diagnosed maladies that were suggested to them on the tube. "Are you tired, run-down, listless? Do you poop out at parties? Are you *unpoopular?*"

PREVIOUS PAGES
Omega Oil—West 147th Street, and Frederick Douglass, Harlem, New York City. Taken March 1997. Ad circa 1910. Hung in NYHS Exhibition.

Lucille Ball and Desi Arnaz nailed it back in the 1950s. The problem "back in the day" (I promised myself I would use this meme only once) was that there was very little regulatory measures for these "medications."

The origins of the Food and Drug Administration, the U.S. federal government's "oldest comprehensive consumer protection agency," can be traced back to about 1848 with the appointment of Lewis Caleb Beck to the Patent Office. Beck carried out chemical analyses of agricultural products, a function that was inherited in 1862 by the newly created Department of Agriculture. Not known by its present name until 1930, "the FDA's modern regulatory functions began with the passage of the 1906 Pure Food and Drugs Act, a law a quarter-century in the making that prohibited interstate commerce in adulterated and misbranded food and drugs."[22]

Don't you feel more at ease now? Here we have the root of the word disease. One can be diagnosed with a life-threatening illness and still feel "at ease" with one's self. We are *not* our disease.

We *are* our ease. For some time now, especially in gay publications like the *Advocate* or on subway billboards in target neighborhoods, there would be advertisements for AIDS medications about which "you should ask your doctor." Sustiva was one of them. Having personally sat in focus groups to name antiretroviral drugs in the early 2000s, I know the power of a brand name's influence on your desire to take that drug. Sustiva. Sustain Life. One of the side effects of Sustiva is "wild, hallucinatory dreams." After falling through the fabric of my bed into an unknown dimension every night, I knew this was not the medication that would allow me to be adherent. What was astounding was I started receiving instant messages from younger people of Gay AOL chat rooms who knew I was HIV-positive asking if I wanted to sell them my Sustiva because it had fast become the latest party drug. OMG! NO! NO!

Since flushing these toxic medications down the toilet hurts the fish in the ocean, I'd recycled them through donor programs when they made me irrational—at best, suicidal, and, at worst,

starting to present with lipodystrophic-acquired disorders characterized by either complete or partial lack of adipose tissue (lipoatrophy).[23] Over the last twenty-one years, I've become a virtual clinical study in both the deleterious and beneficial effects of AIDS medications. Living as long as I have with this virus, I've tried every imaginable AIDS medication, from antiretrovirals to protease-inhibitors.

Fortunately now, the most benign and minimal amount of chemical agents keeps "my virus" at non-detectable levels. In 1999, a doctor who was conducting a drug trial suggested no medications at all. After a year's round of self-injections with interleukin-2, my T-cells, the immune cells that fight disease, started rebounding at levels only Superman could possess. The stuff was like kryptonite. So the next step in this experiment was "a drug holiday," which in the '70s meant a whole different thing. Of course, this process was closely monitored by medical professionals at the esteemed New York Hospital–Cornell Medical Center on York Avenue within a block or so of the Mecca Cigarettes ads (page 90), which I visited on my daily walks to the clinic. A week into my "drug holiday"—a total cessation of my AIDS meds—the expected outcome was that my viral load would increase dramatically and then decrease on its own. As expected, my levels shot up to about ten thousand viral particles per unit. Within six weeks, my viral counts were way up over two million, and my preciously nurtured and cultivated T-cells began to disappear to the lowest levels yet measured.

Within a few weeks, upon receiving a rectal cancer diagnosis in August 2000, I quit the study to have the lentil-sized "mass" surgically removed. In the hospital waiting rooms, there were medical journals with advertisements of different chemotherapies for breast and cervical cancers. After undergoing vicious and barbaric rounds of chemotherapy and radiation treatments, I was left with third-degree burns to my groin that left permanent scarring and suffered permanent hearing loss and tinnitus from *Cisplatin*

ototoxicity.[24] Just last week, I heard there is now a shortage of this cancer treatment.

With all this said and done, perhaps I would have fared better with a dose of Dr. Tucker's 59 for All Pain (page 55). At least I would have gotten a good buzz instead of this incessant ringing in my ears. What a royal pain in the ass that all was, but I'm glad that bit of history is behind me now. Ba-ddum-bum. So much for the "wonders of modern medicine." Concurrently, I am still here in spite of and as a result of modern science.

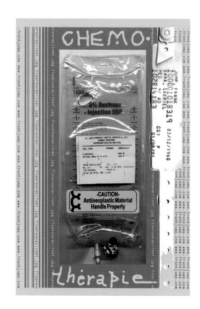

Fluoruracil Chemotherapy Bag and Hospital Bracelet Collage/ID Card. January 2001.

Caroline Rance, the writer of the blog *The Quack Doctor*, discusses Omega Oil's secret ingredients:

The miraculous little green herb was possibly henbane, but fortunately it was in very small quantities—the main ingredients were chloroform, oil of wintergreen and mineral oil. Oil of wintergreen (methyl salicylate) is still a component of deep-heat liniments today and I imagine that sufferers did feel the benefit of this sweet-smelling emerald liquid. It got on the wrong side of the FDA in 1942, when it was judged misbranded because of the exaggerated claims, but this didn't kill off the product—it is still available in some countries today.[25]

Omega Oil was the first fading ad that I ever photographed. I don't remember noticing ghost signs before this. A friend from my photography class called me up and asked if I would walk with him through Harlem to photograph friezes and other architectural details since I had lived there before and he wasn't comfortable walking with his camera alone. When I

Watercolor of Omega Oil. *Courtesy of Sandra Walker, RI.*

noticed the sign, I asked Arthur if he had seen other signs like this before. Terms like ghost signs were not in my lexicon. I was a novice. I quickly climbed the construction scaffolding that still surrounded the newly built police department precinct building that was adjacent to this emerald beauty. Before the cops came out to yell at me to climb down, I got this shot.

What was unimaginable at the time was the kaleidoscopic journey on which this sign would take me, from scouring the five boroughs with Vincenzo in 1997, to a 1999 cross-country road trip that would have me sleeping on the floors and couches in the homes of journalist and ghost signs author Wm. Stage and Tod Swormstedt (American Sign Museum). This sign afforded me the invaluable and instructive collaborations with other urban archaeologists like Kevin Walsh (*Forgotten New York*) and Walter Grutchfield (*14th to 42nd Street*). Who would have thought that I'd become acquainted with Julian Seery

Gude,[26] the great-great-grandson of outdoor media giant and pioneer O.J. Gude, through the digital medium of the Internet if I hadn't found Omega Oil on the day I began my search for a photographic subject.

Another fortunate outcome of discovering this sign was receiving generous attention from journalists around the globe. In May 1999, the *London Observer* did a lovely two-page spread that got the attention of an expatriate American photorealist watercolorist living in London, Sandra Walker, R.I.,[27] whose works are "represented in numerous public and private collections and embassies throughout the world." In 2003, I received a wonderful and unexpected card in the mail from the "internationally renowned artist," who paints watercolors of city scenes, including fading ads. Walker wrote to me about how in 1999, a friend had sent her a newspaper clipping from the *Observer*, and that my photography mirrored the work she does in watercolor. Walker had gone to Harlem in search of the Omega Oil building, found it and painted it. Walker said, "I just wanted to thank you for the inspiration."[28]

Perhaps what has made this image so enduring for me is the actual endurance of the ad itself. Omega Oil is still standing tall, in all its emerald splendor, a tireless beacon that continues to illuminate our remedial and commercial past. This one may just outlive us all.

SYRUP OF FIGS

"So. Are you regular?" A question only an alterkaker[29] would understand. Quite literally, this means "old shitter" in Yiddish. This often overheard question made by our grandparents and aunts and uncles while sitting at the dais of a wedding or bar mitzvah can be considered small talk to some, unmentionable to others. While thumbing carefully through a vintage turn-of-the-century magazine, you will notice an abundance of ads for products to help you go a little easier. One would think that constipation was a much bigger problem back then, or perhaps people seemed much more at ease about talking about their bowel movement or "unmovement."

On a website called *The Museum of Menstruation*, there's a tongue-in-cheek anecdote taken from a 1904 women's medical journal called "The 20th Century Song Book": "Menstrual, kidney & liver problems, constipation & bowels, tiredness, indigestion,

OPPOSITE
Syrup of Figs—Greenpoint Avenue (near corner of Franklin Street), Brooklyn. Taken March 1998. Ad circa 1900s. Hung in NYHS Exhibition.

colic, colds, chills, fever, childbirth, rheumatism, arthritis, menarche, leuchorrhea, dizziness, pain, headache, Cardui, Wine of Cardui, tonic, 'female weakness,' etc."[30]

Perhaps this should be sung to a popular "list song" tune like the "Twelve Days of Christmas" or Billy Joel's "We Didn't Start the Fire." At first I thought Syrup of Figs was a dessert topping. I stood corrected when one of my readers e-mailed me that this was a remedy for constipation and was the main ingredient in Fletcher's Castoria as well. This was a big "a-ha moment" for me. Google Images has quite a collection of marvelous ads for the sweet viscous extract, mostly all claiming to be made from California figs. The etymological root for the word "syrup" actually comes from the Arabic *sharab* (beverage) via the Latin *siropus*. According to Wiktionary, syrup of figs is a laxative and the Cockney rhyming slang is "a wig,"[31] which brings up my childhood hysteria over "Merkin Hall."

As a kid, hemorrhoid commercials were equally hilarious to me. Not so funny anymore. An Israeli MD claims on his website that "hemorrhoids are the consequence of the sitting defecation posture."[32] After 150 years of sitting, the "sitting toilet bowl" has caused physical damage. Apparently, physiologically we were meant to squat. Our diets over 150 years ago were much less processed, and we did get our daily dose of dietary fiber, depending on where you lived and, of course, what you ate. I recall Archie Bunker yelling at Edith on *All in the Family*, "I don't need roughage! I need smoothage!" As American consumers, we are obsessed with what we eat and what we don't eat. The big push (no pun intended) for adding dietary fiber to our diets is over a century old. On a government website sponsored by the National Institute of Health, the benefits for individuals who eat dietary fiber are provided:

Significantly lower risk for developing coronary heart disease, stroke, hypertension, diabetes, obesity, and certain gastrointestinal diseases [and] *lowers blood pressure and serum cholesterol levels. Increased intake of soluble fiber improves glycemia and insulin sensitivity in non-diabetic and diabetic individuals. Fiber supplementation in obese individuals significantly enhances weight loss* [and] *benefits a number of gastrointestinal disorders including the following: gastroesophageal reflux disease, duodenal ulcer, diverticulitis, constipation, and hemorrhoids…More effective communication and consumer education is required to enhance fiber consumption from foods or supplements.*[33]

Perhaps this abstract is a bit more than you can chew, but the trend in American diets is inching bit by bit (or bite by bite) toward eating better than we have in the past one hundred years. Organic, whole foods are not just brand names but have become a desired option for more people who can afford to eat better. We all can afford to eat better, but not everyone has the means or proper dietary education. First Lady Michelle Obama has recently piloted the Let's Move campaign, aimed at helping end the problem of childhood obesity by "Creating a healthy start for children; Empowering parents and caregivers; Providing healthy food in schools; Improving access to healthy, affordable foods; Increasing physical activity."[34]

The school where I teach has a cooking workshop for second graders that teaches them how to prepare simple yet healthy snacks like black bean salsa, guacamole and fruit salads—all with adult supervision, of course. Ideally, when they go home with the recipes and the steps for making the snacks, they can share them with their parents. Every time you turn on the TV, open your laptop or walk out your door, you're being asked to make a food choice, so they may as well be good choices. Aren't you hungry for…*something* now?

FLETCHER'S CASTORIA

Children cry for Fletcher's.

With the original intent to be seen by people crossing the Manhattan Bridge over Chinatown, this sign was clearly visible from the D train until its demise over a decade ago. In 1999, when I first launched the campaign website, I was informed by fading ads enthusiast Barbara Roberts that Castoria was not a castor oil at all but a prune-flavored laxative for children. Roberts informed me the ingredients were cascara sagrada, syrup of figs and extract of prunes.

Remnants of Castoria ads still pepper the five boroughs and are by far one of the more commonly seen vintage ads in New York City, from the Bowery to Jamaica, Queens. Chris Riley wrote to me in

Fletcher's Castoria—Market and Henry Streets, Chinatown, New York City. Taken March 1997. Ad circa 1900s. Hung in NYHS Exhibition.

May 2000 that Fletcher's Castoria was manufactured by Charles Henry Fletcher beginning in 1871 and had been patented in 1868. The initial patent for Castoria included "senna, sodium bicarbonate, essence of wintergreen, taraxicum, sugar, and water." Riley said it was modified later to include other things like pumpkin, anise and wormseed to improve the taste to be more like root beer.

Within months of the website launching, I was contacted by the Centaur Company, which still owns the patent for Castoria, and asked if we could trade links. For more information about Castoria products, visit the Centaur Company website![35]

RADWAY'S READY RELIEF

Perhaps Radway's Ready Relief is a precursor to today's pain-management addiction problems, as can be seen in this sales promotion for the cure-all that started out with a patriotic pill-popping pitch in the *New York Times* on October 23, 1861:

A FREE GIFT; TO THE AMERICAN PEOPLE. WHAT THE FEDERAL TROOPS ARE FIGHTING TO SUSTAIN. HOW OUR SOLDIERS SHOULD BE PREPARED TO FIGHT. DRS. RADWAY & CO. RADWAY & CO., NO. 23 John-st., New-York.

HOW OUR SOLDIERS SHOULD BE PREPARED TO FIGHT. Health and discipline are the most important elements. RADWAY'S READY RELIEF. IN DR. RADWAY'S REMEDIES RADWAY'S

READY RELIEF IN HIS KNAPSACK, WHEN SICK, DUTY OF CIVILIANS. ARMY INDORSEMENT. NOT ONE IN THE HOSPITAL.

IMPORTANT TO FAMILIES. DR. RADWAY'S PILLS. RADWAY'S REGULATING PILLS RADWAY'S RENOVATING RESOLVENT. IT CURES, WITH ASTONISHING RAPIDITY. HUMORS AND SORES OF ALL KINDS, LADIES NOTICE.[36]

Two years later, this early "info-mercial" appeared in the *New York Times* touting new medical benefits and cures with an apparent topical application of this miraculous medication:

A New Method of Curing Certain Diseases, by the Use of Radway's Ready Relief

Has been recently discovered, and is calculated to supersede the use of all electro-magnetic machines, external applications, liniments, plasters, emenagogues, medicines for fever and ague, rheumatism, paralysis, numbness, neuralgia, &c. The application is simple, the effects pleasant, and the cure positive and infallible. It proves what we have for nearly a quarter of a century maintained, that Radway's Ready Relief is the best, quickest, and most important remedial agent ever discovered. It is, however, only recently that we have discovered its immense curative power in certain diseases by this new process.

THE SECRET OF ITS APPLICATION was suggested to us by Professor Reid, Professor and Lecturer of Chemistry for

ABOVE LEFT
Radway's Ready Relief—Delancey Street, New York City. Taken August 1997. Ad circa 1890s.

ABOVE RIGHT
Radway's close-up.

many years in the New-York College of Physicians, the New-York Hospitals, Edinburgh University, &c., &c. We have tried it in a number of cases that had previously resisted all other treatments. Every case yielded with astonishing rapidity. The success of the Ready Relief, in its ordinary application, has been greater than all other remedies in use. This can be vouched for by thousands who have used it.

Let those afflicted with the following complaints use it under the new method, and we guarantee an immediate cure: RHEUMATISM, NEURALGIA, Gout, Sciatica, Nervousness, Fever and Ague, INDIGESTION, SMALL POX, MEASLES. Cramps, Spasms, Lumbago, Headache, Heart Disease, FEMALE COMPLAINTS, Retention, Suppressions, or Misplaced Menstruation, URINAL ORGANS, Diseases of the Kidneys, Bladder, Urethra, Weakness, Spermatorrhea, Pains, Aches, Spasms in the Back, Thighs, Hips, &c. THE APPLICATION in these cases must be made TO THE SPINE.

Rub the entire length of the spine and across the small of the back with RADWAY'S READY RELIEF for ten or fifteen minutes, night and morning, and a cure will follow. We do not recommend its application in this form as an experiment, but with a full knowledge that it will cure either of the above-named complaints.

We are recommending no new or untried medicine—its merit and efficacy as a specific for many of the pains, aches and infirmities that afflict mankind, is acknowledged by thousands—but suggest to our readers and patients a new method of its application for certain complaints, which, if followed, will insure a more positive and rapid cure than any known treatment in vogue. In all cases ask for RADWAY'S READY RELIEF. Patients are invited to call at Dr. RADWAY'S Medical Office, No. 87 Maiden-lane, New-York. RADWAY'S RELIEF is sold by Druggists.[37]

There was a spine-tingling jingle that went with this pain medication and cure-all with lyrics and sheet music published in 1883 (at right).

No wonder this cure-all was so popular, with all those claimed medicinal benefits! Currently, I'm working on having this jingle re-created by singers with HIV by the fall of 2011. I can hear those bass ba-ba-ba-bas sung with ecstatic exuberance already.

As sung by the Apollo Club, of Boston
Radway's Ready Relief (from Paine) Male Quartet with Bass solo

Twenty years of sleepless nights,
Twenty years of sleepless nights,

William Sydney Myers, Myers
Esah of Havana Cuba, Of Havana
Cuba, Cuba, ba, ba, ba, ba,
Cuba, Cuba,

The correspondent of the Times,
The London Times
The London, London Times.
Suffer'd with acute and chronic rheumatiz,
Acute, acute
Acute and chronic rheumatiz

For five and twenty years he had not enjoy'd one whole nights calm rest
One night's calm rest.

Radway's Read Relief,
Radway's Read Relief,

He applied,
It immediately gave him rest
And secur'd him the first calm
And undisturbed sleep during the twenty years
The continued use of Radway's Relief cured him
Radways Ready Relief,
Always ask for
Radways Ready Relief,
Take no other!

Price per bottle twenty-five cents,
Radway, Radway, Radway, Radway,
Only, oh! Only,
Utterly Too cheap! Cheap!

And for sale, for sale, ev'rywhere
Radways Ready Relief,
O always ask for Radways Ready Relief,
Radways Ready Relief,
Ev'rywhere for sale by all apothecaries
All apothecaries in the land,
Including Chelsea Beach,

O always ask for Radway's Ready Relief
Ev'rywhere for sale by all apothecaries
All apothecaries in the land,
Including Chelsea Beach,

Ask for Radway's Ready Relief,
His Ready Relief

Radway's ready relief: Male quartet with bass solo By John Knowles Paine

AMAROSA SCALP RUB

For Your Hair

Another fading ad under the EL along Broadway in Brooklyn—a veritable treasure-trove of signs of life from Brooklyn's commercial past. On a walking tour that I had co-sponsored with the Brooklyn Historical Society during my show at the Williamsburg Art & Historical Center, along with Kevin Walsh's *Forgotten New York* crew, we took a large number of people down Broadway.[39]

(?) OIL—CURES SORE THROAT

Another snake oil that claimed to "cure sore throat as soon as applied. For sale by druggist." The red-and-white holding tank in the distance was one of two that were known as the Elmhurst gas tanks, a popular landmark, often mentioned in traffic reports on the radio. KeySpan (now National Grid Energy) dismantled the twin tanks in 2002 for the construction of a new community park.[40]

DAVID BLUSTEIN & BROTHER FOR RAW FURS & GINSENG

Here is an example of the business address marker as ad. This form of storefront sign was common in the garment district and other areas of New York City, where the simple "sign above your store" was impossible given the immensity of these buildings and the large population and diversity of businesses within. Along the length of some buildings, you will see the traces of these address markers on every floor. Walter Grutchfield's website encompasses

LEFT
Amarosa Scalp Rub—Broadway, Williamsburg, Brooklyn. Taken August 1997. Ad circa 1900s.

MIDDLE
(?) Oil—Cures Sore Throat—Williamsburg, Brooklyn. Taken August 1997. Ad circa 1900s.

RIGHT
David Blustein & Brother for Raw Furs and Ginseng— Seventh Avenue, New York City. Taken March 1998. Ad circa 1910.

the Garment District, and you can see a multitude of these markers and his excellent documentation of them.

At the top you see Photo-Stemmerman. Below that is a name I can't make out, but directly under it, it says MFG (manufacturing) FURRIERS. Right below that it says "Karp Bros. Coats & Suits." But clear as day it says "David Blustein & Brother for Raw Furs & Ginseng" below that.

This Blustein remnant of the later years of the Far East trade was documented on the authority of Grutchfield with the following details:

David Blustein & Bro. was founded around 1905 by the brothers David Blustein and Isadore Blustein. Isadore Blustein (1868–192?) was the older brother who lived in West Virginia (David Blustein & Bro. had an office in Charleston) from as early as 1907 until at least the mid-1920s…David Blustein (1874–1932) was born in Triski, Russia, immigrated in 1891, was naturalized (in Charleston, West Virginia) in 1896, lived in Manhattan (West End Ave. in 1920) and later on Long Island

(Hempstead in 1930). The business was located here at 158–164 W. 27th St. from 1913 until 1948. In 1940 the name was changed to Blustein Furs… This refers to the branch office in Charleston, West Virginia, and to exporting ginseng and other botanical roots.[41] A photograph sent to me by Dennis A. Stone, a grandson of David Blustein, shows David (the man at the far right) and two other men gazing at a large pile of ginseng…In 1945 Dennis Stone's father was serving in the U.S. Army in Frankfurt, Germany, when he annotated this price list of Blustein offerings for raw furs. The annotation reads, "I was in contact with my office by cable and air mail. I wrote this price list from Frankfort." Dennis notes, "He was apparently running the business in 1945 while serving in the Army." The verso expands on various offers, including prices for ginseng.

…Photo Stemmerman at the top refers to the Stemmerman Photo Craft Laboratories located here from 1913 to 1918. William H. Stemmerman

(1867–1951) was a druggist and physician in Passaic, New Jersey, and the original Stemmerman Photo-craft Laboratories was located in that city from around 1911. Stemmerman retired from his businesses before 1920. (He appears in the US Census of 1920 living in Pasadena, Calif. with employment listed as "none.") The New York branch of the photo lab re-located to the east 20s in 1918, and Joseph G. Taylor (1891/92–?) became the owner. In the early 1930s the name changed to Taylor Photo Co.[42]

It was not uncommon to see companies advertising constituent products for a final larger product as you see in signs for "coat fronts" and here for raw furs. It is surprising to see ginseng sold next to animal furs. I've often wondered about the history of this trade. Not surprisingly, many of the things we traded came from China. Today, goods produced and bought from the Chinese are driving our whole consumer economy, which to some is a blessing and others a curse. American consumers enjoy lower prices for goods while American producers are literally digging for ginseng. What's fascinating is it all began with furs and ginseng. On the *JSTOR Plant* website, a bit of history and etymology of ginseng is offered:

Ginseng enters the English and French vocabularies in the ages of exploration. In the French as early as 1750, in English in 1654, and for Portuguese, the term ginsao appeared even earlier (Holmes, 283). In Chinese, 人蔘 (phonetically rénshēn) is the name for ginseng and that roughly translates as "man root." Even the Chinese character 人 is meant to look like a man with two legs. So there you have it. A little linguistic lesson for the day.

So, the ginseng trade has been well established for centuries and has turned a tidy profit for many, including that beacon of 19th century New York City life, John Jacob Astor. Astor was one of the more ambitious people ever to set foot on American soil. Astor, German by birth, landed in the United States in 1784 just at the end of the Revolutionary War, immediately established himself in the fur trade with Quebec, and became incredibly wealthy. Not being content relying on middlemen, Astor bought his own ship for sending his furs to London, learned of the East India Company trade with China, and immediately capitalized in the Chinese demand for furs.[43]

Hard to imagine that this woody root—once used as an aphrodisiac and currently used as a mild organic stimulant in alternative energy drinks, with claims to countless other benefits—was also the root of New York's trade with China. Apparently, George Washington had heard about the Chinese need for ginseng and learned there was a huge supply growing indigenously in North America. Since the only crop we could grow that would be valuable to the Chinese at the time was ginseng, which wasn't being used widely in the United States, it became a valued U.S. export. On a Chinese cultural website, the following historical facts were provided:

Ginseng helped promote the formation of the notion of international trade in the US. The entire country was connected to trade with China. Not only merchants in New York, Boston and Philadelphia, but isolated farmers in deep mountains had learned that they could be paid by something grown in the northern slope of the mountains. About the same time when the Empress of China unloaded the Ginseng at China, George Washington (1732–1799) met some people who were doing Ginseng business in Virginia. He recorded it in his diary, "I met numbers of Persons & Pack horses going in with Ginseng: & for salt & other articles at the Market Below."[44]

In today's market, there is still a great demand for ginseng. Although our more lucrative exports lay in automobiles and other technology, China produces its own. In the American producer's dig for a *new* ginseng, let's hope the only commodity left to trade with China isn't just our national debt.

DR. TUCKER'S 59 FOR ALL PAIN

This sign on Broadway in the Bushwick section of Brooklyn advertises a turn-of-the-century pain medication. On the corner is a business marker for S. Huffman—Jeweler & Optician. Recently in Park Slope, Brooklyn, another Dr. Tucker's sign was revealed while a restaurant called Sidecar was renovating its space. Brothers John and Bart DeCoursy had this to say about their summer of 2007 discovery on their website:

When the brothers first signed the lease on 560 5th Ave, they had no idea that a gem lay waiting to be discovered. As they transformed the building from a children's clothing store into a restaurant, they pulled back layer upon layer of wallpaper and sheetrock in search of exposed brick. Instead, they found what looked like the letter A. They furiously scraped the wall down until the whole image was on display: "DR. TUCKER'S 59 CURES COUGHS, COLDS. FOR ALL PAIN." Since they wanted a classic decor that would feel warm and comfortable, they knew immediately that it would be incorporated into the design. With a little research, they found that Dr. Tucker's 59 was a popular elixir during the late 1800's and was eventually taken off the shelves in the early 1900's due to the fact that its main ingredient, cocaine, had been outlawed. Seen as a sign from above that the boys had found the right location, they incorporated this beautiful work of art into their logo; Sidecar—Food & Drink Cures All Pain. Eventually, Bart also created a cocktail in its honor. All of the present cocktails' ingredients, however, are perfectly safe and legal.[45]

I'll drink to that!

OPPOSITE
Dr. Tucker's 59 for All Pain—
Brooklyn's Broadway Elevated J Line.
Taken June 1998. Ad circa 1900s.

Days with Art

Lingering in Frank Jump's Images

The poignancy in Frank Jump's chosen subject matter, his disappearing ads, transforms the language of advertising into a poetics of signs. And there is nothing forgettable about either the images or Frank's inspired pursuit of art, and of living. One thinks of Atget's photographs of the façades and storefronts in a disappearing Paris, but Jump's compositions are decidedly less formal. Or perhaps it can be said that there is still room to breathe in Jump's images, as Atget's are sealed off (if brilliantly so).

Much has been made of the connections between Jump's photographs and his own biography. Both elucidate the culture of a specific moment. Both survive, beautifully so, even surrounded by loss. Both are deeply inspiring. One work that continues to hold me is the triptych Confrontation (Dr. Tucker's 59 for All Pain).[46] It documents an advertisement painted in white text on brown, forming a banner running the length of a windowless brick building. Read left to right, the three photographs shift from sunlight-heightened contrast to an overcast, slow fadedness and ultimately include the elevated subway track, underscoring the proximity of the building (and

photographer) to the approaching train. In the last, Jump has shifted the color of the clouds and the sign to an impossible luminosity. In each, the presence of 59 and PAIN and the sometimes legible FOR ALL form an unshakeable chant, not unlike the raps and beat poetry Jump composed for the early days of ACT UP.

With the generosity and leadership of artists, Visual AIDS utilizes visual art to promote dialogue about HIV. We document the work of HIV-positive artists and pay tribute to the creative contributions of AIDS activism—and we are proud to honor the extraordinary photography of Frank Jump.

After almost a decade of attempting to fathom and alter the human devastation, in 1989, Visual AIDS inaugurated a Day Without Art. Early exhibitions of Jump's Fading Ad Campaign were part of a shift in this landmark art action that coincided with the World Health Organization's AIDS Awareness Day on December 1. Originally, the day was to be a cultural intervention: shrouding works of art and darkening the galleries in the face of the AIDS crisis. The gestures were resonant. Tom Sokolowski, a founding member of Visual AIDS, described the event's importance to the

Dr. Tucker's 59 for All Pain—up on elevated train track, confronted by conductor. Taken March 1999.

New York Times: "The language of art speaks in different ways from normal discourse. Perhaps those of us who are engaged in the making and displaying of works of art can in some way use the medium to dispel ignorance and bigotry that have surrounded what began simply as a medical problem." After the advent of drug therapies that extended the lives of those who had access, it became more urgent to share the creative contributions of HIV-positive artists. Jump's show at the Gershwin Gallery in 1997 and his 2000 exhibition at the Williamsburg Art and Historical Center were leading examples of a new Day With[out] Art.

Like the Visual AIDS Archive Project, in which he is a long-standing artist member, Frank Jump's art practice creates a record of ephemeral histories. Even without the awareness of his roots in formative New York gay and AIDS activism, it's impossible not to characterize Frank as innately collaborative. At the height of publicity and interest in Fading Ad, Frank took the opportunity to speak about HIV. He has always been open about his longtime survivor status and was instrumental in linking his photographs with the message that "AIDS is not over."

It's worth mentioning that Jump's early adoption of the web to share his photographs

challenged an individualized idea of art and
the singular, marketable, finite work of the
artist. When Frank opened the Fading Ad
Gallery in Brooklyn in the mid-2000s, he
programmed exhibitions of various Visual AIDS
Archive Project members, and not just on Day
With[out] Art but year round. And through it
all, there are the photographs. Like a private
moment in a public space, the image of 59 for
All Pain sometimes lingers on with me for days.
Holding this image is an active experience. It
is one of the things art can do, and particularly
in Frank Jump's hands, as he does it so lovingly
and so well.

Amy Sadao
Executive Director, Visual AIDS
August 1, 2010, New York

Food,
Snacks and
Candy

HAMS AND CAPOCOLLI

One hundred and twenty five years before this sign was painted in its block sans serif lettering, the navy yard was a bustling harbor where merchant vessels were built. Earlier still in the 1630s, Wallabout Bay was the site where the first French-speaking Walloon settlers from the Netherlands relocated. It was from this very early Dutch settlement that the city of Brooklyn sprang forth. Embedded in shores of this waterfront is a fascinating and gruesome history of colonial skirmishes with the Canarsee Indians, the cultivation of the first tobacco plantations in the New World and the British mooring their prison ships during the American Revolution, throwing over ten thousand American soldiers who died of neglect overboard to decay on the Wallabout Basin beaches.[47]

This sign stared west over the Brooklyn Navy Yard for almost a century to witness the navy yard's height of activity during World War II, when over seventy thousand people were employed. Hams and Capocolli also witnessed the goings-on at the notorious JJ's Navy Yard Cocktail Lounge just a couple of blocks south on Flushing and Washington Avenues. The lounge seems to have been there forever and is the subject of some Brooklynites' bravado stories, according to Nicole Brydson: "Dubbed everything from secret stripper bar to the scariest bar in Brooklyn, neighbors often wear a visit to this dive, on the corner of Washington and Flushing Avenues, like a badge of honor; the bar as portal to a forgotten yesteryear."[48]

Ham production is documented to have originated between 300 and 400 BC during the Roman times.[49] Prosciutto ham and capocolli are cured meats popular in Italian sandwiches called panini.

PREVIOUS PAGES
Hams & Capocolli/Wallabout Provisions Co.—Brooklyn Navy Yard. Taken September 1997. Incorporated from July 28, 1925, through October 31, 1933. Hung in NYHS Exhibition.

OPPOSITE
Watercolor of Hams & Capocolli. *Courtesy of Sandra Walker, RI.*

A single sandwich is called a panino. In the United States, they are known as cold cuts, and in earlier days they were considered meat "provisions," since they were ready-made and had a long shelf life due to the curing process that preserves the meat. In Brooklyn, the slang term for a capocola (singular) is gabagool, which derives from the Neapolitan accent and other southern Italian and Sicilian dialects.[50] Vincenzo insists on pronouncing capocola with his Torinese accent. Not a grinder or sub goes past his lips without at least a few slices of the sweet and the hot dry capocolli in combination, and to this day it is one of his favorite sandwiches (and this one of his favorite ads). This ad also caught the eye of my friend Sandra Walker, who created this watercolor based on the photograph, which for me as an artist is the highest form of flattery.

From the height of this ad, Hams and Capocolli could have also spied the goings-on at the Cumberland Packing Company, which is just a few blocks south.

SWEET'N LOW

Everyone in my family tells this story, but everyone starts it in a different way. My mother starts it in the diner across from the Brooklyn Navy Yard, where my grandfather Benjamin Eisenstadt, a short-order cook, invented the sugar packet and Sweet'N Low, and with them built the fortune that would be the cause of all the trouble.

—Rich Cohen[51]

Everyone I know has a story about the pink packet, especially if you are from Flatbush. I didn't start out in Brooklyn though. Usually after a few beers, I'll admit I'm from Queens, famous for its…diners! As early as I can remember, on every table in every diner, there was a rectangular glass container filled with an assortment of sweeteners. I never knew people actually bought Sweet'N Low. As a kid, when going out to the Crossbay Diner with the families of friends, invariably I would witness with horror their grandmother surreptitiously dumping loads of the pink packets into her unsnapped clamshell pocketbook, her eyes darting back and forth, looking to see if anyone was spying on her grand pink theft as she snapped her purse closed. So when I noticed the product on grocery store shelves, it seemed odd that anyone would actually buy it. When I first drove by the Cumberland Packing Company along the Brooklyn Navy Yard on Flushing Avenue, I imagined thousands of old ladies with their pocketbooks grabbing what they could while quickly ambling down the aisles of warehouse shelves. Could make for a great marketing strategy. Instead of winning a year's supply on *The Price Is Right*, you could win "A five-minute trip through the Cumberland Packing Company, Home of Sweet'N Low!" Five minutes alone in the factory and all you can stuff in your purse—a grandmother's dream. Now that we're over fifty, I'm continually mortified as Vincenzo stuffs a few pink packets into his shirt pocket before leaving a restaurant, although sometimes—he steals the salt shaker.

Not very long after I took this shot, the Cumberland Packing Company painted a new Sweet'N Low ad, covering the lovely cursive script and block serif lettering of "The Perfect Sugar Substitute." The newer ad is a bit disappointing in its style, but subconsciously, it seems aesthetically justifiable to me, since there really is "no perfect sugar substitute." Back in the day, the options were limited to saccharine or cyclamates. The cyclamates scare and subsequent ban of the early 1960s is etched into my consumer DNA. I can remember packages of Funny Face drink mix touting "no cyclamates"[52] as I went shopping for groceries with my mom at Bohack's on Merrick Boulevard in Laurelton, Queens.

OPPOSITE
Sweet'n Low—the Perfect Sugar Substitute. In back of the Cumberland Packing Company. Brooklyn Navy Yard. Taken May 1997 Ad circa early 1950s. Hung in NYHS Exhibition.

I've often wondered what ever happened to cyclamates, since they seem to have faded from the American consumer consciousness. On the Elmhurst College website, the history of this sweetener was provided by Professor Charles E. Ophardt:

Michael Sveda, while a graduate student at the University of Illinois, discovered cyclamate by smoking a cigarette. While working on the synthesis of anti-pyretic (anti-fever) drugs in the laboratory in 1937, he put his cigarette down on the lab bench. When he put it back in his mouth, he discovered the sweet taste of cyclamate (unsanitary lab technique).

Cyclamate was initially marketed as tablets that were recommended for use as a tabletop sweetener for diabetics. In 1958, cyclamates were classified as GRAS (Generally Recognized as Safe). A mixture of cyclamate and saccharin, which had been found to have synergistic sweetening properties and improved taste, was subsequently marketed for use in special dietary foods. In the 1950's diet drinks were introduced using a cyclamate/saccharin blend. The market grew rapidly and soon accounted for about 30% of the soft drink sales.

In 1969, the result of a chronic toxicity study with a mixture of cyclamate and

saccharin was interpreted as implicating cyclamate as a bladder carcinogen in rats. Cyclamate was removed from GRAS status and eventually in 1970 banned in the United States from use in foods, beverages and drugs, and is still currently banned. However, many other countries did not act on this incomplete data, and cyclamate continued to be used as a sweetener in those countries. Today over 55 countries have approved the use of cyclamate.[53]

So cyclamates are alive and well and living in food products around the globe—just not here in the United States. Apparently, there's been a lot of controversy over saccharine in the last few years, and according to Rich Cohen, the Sweet'N Low family has had their hand in it. Here is another excerpt from Rich Cohen's "bittersweet" family story:

My father starts the story in downtown Brooklyn, in the courtroom where my Uncle Marvin, the first son of the patriarch, a handsome, curly-haired man who insists on being called Uncle Marvelous, is facing off against federal

prosecutors. After assuming control of the Cumberland Packing Company, which makes Sweet'N Low, Sugar in the Raw, Nu-Salt, and Butter Buds, Marvin, among other things that caused a scandal, put a criminal on the payroll, a reputed associate of the Bonanno crime family. That criminal made illegal campaign contributions to Senator Alfonse D'Amato, who sponsored legislation that kept saccharin on the market. Saccharin, a key ingredient of Sweet'N Low, had been found to cause cancer. In the end, Marvin cut a deal with prosecutors, testifying for the government and keeping himself out of prison.[54]

Never could I imagine so much controversy and drama over a food additive. Oops. I forgot about red dye #2. In a 2008 *Newsweek* article about the five top controversial food additives, another sweetener that goes by the brand name Splenda, otherwise known as sucralose (acesulfame potassium), makes that list.[55] But for the sake of brevity, let's stick to one sweet scandal at a time, and this one's a saccharine story to say the least. On the NPR website

that is currently featuring Rich Cohen's book *Sweet and Low*, it goes into detail about the sweet deal that was made with the FDA and its attempt to ban the pink stuff:

Saccharin was discovered in 1879, and was used during both world wars to sweeten foods, helping to compensate for sugar shortages and rationing. It is 300 times sweeter than sugar. In 1977, a Canadian study that looked specifically at the role of impurities—and of other suspected tumor causes, such as parasites in test animals— showed convincingly that saccharin itself was causing bladder cancer in rats. That same year, FDA proposed to ban saccharin for all uses except as an over-the-counter drug in the form of a tabletop sweetener. Congress responded by passing the Saccharin Study and Labeling Act, which placed a moratorium on any ban of the sweetener while additional safety studies were conducted. The ban was officially lifted in 1991 and saccharin continues to have a fairly large appeal as a tabletop sweetener, particularly in restaurants, where it is available in single-

serving packets under trade names such as Sweet 'n Low. Because it has a good shelf life, saccharin is used widely in fountain sodas, and its stability at high temperatures makes it an option for sweetening baked goods, unlike aspartame, which degrades when heated. Saccharin also is favored economically because it can be made inexpensively. [56]

After a long and protracted attempt to ban saccharine as an artificial sweetener, in 2010, the EPA finally released this cloying statement about this substance:

In the late 1990s, the National Toxicology Program and the International Agency for Research on Cancer re-evaluated the available scientific information on saccharin and its salts and concluded that it is not a potential human carcinogen. Because the scientific basis for remaining on EPA's lists no longer applies, the agency has removed saccharin and its salts from its lists. EPA proposed the removal of saccharin and its salts from the lists on April 22, 2010 and did not receive any comments opposing the proposal. [57]

Phew! I sure feel safer now. There are now so many choices for artificial sweeteners—the pink stuff, the yellow stuff, the blue stuff. Surely you remember the Equal commercials, with Cher so eloquently and glamorously touting that she uses the "Blue Stuff." I always imagined a counter-ad featuring Roseanne for Sugar in the Raw (also packaged at Cumberland factory) with her claim in that Midwest twang, "Heck, I use the Brown Stuff." I've stopped using sugar since my nutritionist told me our bodies (especially mine) convert it almost immediately into triglycerides. Stevia seems to be the latest sweetener craze. Less sugar still is the best sugar substitute, as far as I'm concerned. Childhood obesity and a rise in people becoming diabetic in this country are problems that need to be tackled. Just don't knock me over trying to get to the Sweet'N Low, please.

FULTON STREET FISH MARKET

If I invite some boy some night
To dine on my fine finnan haddie
—Cole Porter

Historically located along the East River in Lower Manhattan just south of the Brooklyn Bridge and only six blocks north of Wall Street, the Fulton Fish Market was one of the oldest continuously running fish markets in the country, second only to the Maine Avenue Market in Washington, D.C. After 180 years of operation in Manhattan, the famous fish market relocated its operations to the Hunts Point in the Bronx on November 14, 2005. According to the New Fulton Fish Market website:

The market first opened on that site in 1807 on land donated to New

Fulton Street Fish Market—New York City. Taken June 1997. Storefront ads circa 1940s.

York City, and at first was a general market for both fish and goods other than fish. In 1822 the fish merchants occupied a new Fulton Fish Market building, located on South Street between Fulton and Beekman Streets.

Prior to 1850, housekeepers from Brooklyn and nearby areas would purchase fish directly from the market. However, since that time, wholesale customers were the primary buyers. The market gradually gained in importance, and in 1924 the market sold 384 million pounds of fish, 25 percent of all seafood sold in the United States

The Fulton Fish market was primarily located in two open air structures, the "Tin Building" and the "New Building," in which various dealers rented stalls from the Port Authority of New York with closed offices at the back of the stalls. The New Building was opened in 1939 by Mayor La Guardia, after pilings of the old market building gave way in 1936 and the entire building slid into the river. Not only was the marketplace old and established, but many of the wholesalers at the Fulton market were well-established firms.[58]

An ultramodern, 400,000-square-foot, fully refrigerated indoor fish market and facility with all the latest amenities, including fish wholesalers, retailers and restaurants, was completed at a cost of $86 million without any loss of employees. The project generated new construction and retail jobs in an economically depressed area in the Bronx while opening up prime real estate in Manhattan for luxury residential housing. One of the unspoken reasons why the fish market moved, other than the smell of fish that permeated the area for over a century, was the stranglehold that organized crime had on the Manhattan market. The new facility is run under the supervision of the City of New York Business Integrity Commission in an attempt to "eliminate organized crime and other forms of corruption and criminality from the industries it regulates." Sounds like a new and more effective organization should be regulating Wall Street, which gives new meaning to the term organized crime.[59]

GRADE A MILK

This "got milk" ad heralds from a time when this part of Brooklyn had the lion's share of dairies. It may seem hard to imagine a pastoral Brooklyn with cows grazing as far as the eye could see, but in its heyday, much of the area's milk was produced along what is now Atlantic Avenue in East New York and along Flushing Avenue alongside the Brooklyn Navy Yard, straight through Bushwick, the most eastern division of Brooklyn. The early Dutch and English settlers of the late seventeenth century in Flatlands raised dairy cows. The following history was provided by a historical resource study prepared by the Department of the Interior on this precursor to western Long Island's nascent dairy industry:

Other Dutch towns, such as Bushwick, and English communities, such as Jamaica, Flushing and those at the eastern end of Long Island, had much larger herds of sheep than the Dutch settlements of the bay. In Flatlands, swine were almost as equally scarce, there being twenty-one in

Grade A Milk—Waverly Place, Clinton Hill, Brooklyn. Taken August 1998. Ad circa 1900s.

1676; Flatbush at that time had fifty-two. Eleven oxen were to be found at Flatlands in 1676 and twenty-five at Flatbush. The main draft animals were horses, both Flatlands and Flatbush having each approximately one hundred horses in 1676.

The most important livestock were cattle. Flatlands reported 209 cows in 1676, and Flatbush. It would appear that Jamaica Bay farmers were as much dairy farmers as growers of crops. This gives special importance to the meadows bordering the bay, since it provided forage for numerous cattle as well as horses. Dankers informs us that the Dutch mowed the salt meadows and moved the hay presumably to their barns. In the same year as the Danker's visit, 1679, horses were grazing on Barren Island. That salt hay was mowed and sold in Brooklyn in 1826 is reported in Baxter's journal. Thus the bay's meadows for two hundred years provided grazing for livestock and cut hay for use at farms in the area and also for sale to others.[60]

Apparently, by the mid-nineteenth century, Brooklyn dairy farmers were faced with a lung plague that afflicted their cattle. According to a report of the commissioner of agriculture for the year 1879:

In 1849, William Meakim of Bushwick, Long Island (New York) kept a large dairy and employed a man with a yoke of oxen in drawing grain from the New York and Brooklyn distilleries. A milkman on the way, who had lung fever in his herd persuaded this man to use his oxen in drawing a dead cow out of his stable. Soon after the oxen sickened and died; and the disease extending to his dairy cows, Mr. Meakim lost forty head in the short space of three months. The stables have thus become infected, Mr. Meakim continued to lose from six to ten cows yearly for the succeeding twenty years, or as long as he kept in the milk business. This, which is but one instance out of a hundred, covers fifteen years of the plague in the Skillman stables, and brings the record down to 1869.[61]

Despite this twenty-year outbreak of bovine pneumonia, by the late 1890s, the Brooklyn dairy businesses had experienced a boom.

Names like Axelrod, Breakstone, Renken, Borden and Sheffield Farms all shared their roots in Brooklyn dairy farms during this time. Many of these dairies were in production until the early 1960s. I remember drinking milk from a bottle from the Renken Dairy as a child. According to Kevin Walsh on his *Forgotten New York* site, the following defunct dairy-related buildings still stand:

R.H. Renken Dairy at SW corner of Classon & Myrtle Avenues, Clinton Hill Brooklyn. [The Art Deco–designed] *Building although presently unused, was constructed in the 1930s by Koch & Wagner. The M.H. Renken Dairy of Brooklyn, NY was established in 1927 in the eastern part of the borough, continuing operation until 1962.*

Sheffield Farms, a major milk distributor in the Northeast in the late 1800s and early 1900s, was acquired by National Dairy Products (now Kraft, Inc.) in 1925. It has left a number of impressive buildings around town, not least what is now the CBS Broadcast Center at 524 West 57th Street at the northern end of Hell's Kitchen.

...Sheffield Farms in Brooklyn. This facility was on south side of Fulton Street between Brooklyn & New York Avenues. The building was transformed to The Restoration Center in the early 1970s. The Restoration center contains retail stores that includes a Duane-Reade drugstore, Baskin-Robbins, a branch of Citibank, a supermarket that was formerly Pathmark, a skating rink and the Billie Holiday Theater where off-off Broadway shows are presented.[62]

Even the lesser-known products like Axelrod's Dairy, established in the late nineteenth century and catering to New York's kosher community, had their headquarters in Brooklyn. In 1930, Axelrod established another branch in Freeport, New York. According to Rabbi Jeffrey A. Marx in a historical outline of the Breakstone (Breghshtein) Brother's Dairy:

It should be noted that Joseph and Isaac's enterprise was, by no means, a novel one. In fact, the history of Axelrod's Dairy is closely parallel to Breakstone Bros.: In 1896, Wolf Axelord had established both a dairy retail store and wholesale distribution business on Madison St. A few years later, he moved his business to Brooklyn, where Axelrod's Dairy sold sour cream, and Pot Cheese products which were delivered by horse and wagon. At some point, Axelrod's began manufacturing their own products, which were produced in up-state NY dairies and then, packed in ice, shipped by train to NY. In 1932, just a few years after Breakstone's Dairy, Axelrod's was also bought out by National Dairy Products Co.[63]

According to Marx, in 1889, Joseph Breakstone was selling milk from 203 Division Street in Williamsburg, Brooklyn. His brother Isaac Breakstone, "still listed as Brekstone," was operating a butter business at 602 Myrtle Avenue in Brooklyn, with other outlets at 3 Wallabout Market, as well as operating other locations in Greenwich Village and Harlem. In 1907, the Breakstone Brothers moved their operation to 3 Washington Avenue (now within the confines of the Brooklyn Navy Yard) and also established locations in Queens.

The W.M. Evans Dairy Co. at 3480 Fulton Street and Eldert Lane in Cypress Hills, Brooklyn (on the Queens border),[64] had, according to Kevin Walsh, "the highest numbered address on Brooklyn's Fulton Street." Who knew Brooklyn was once renowned for its dairy production? Brooklyn is also famous for a local beverage documented as having originated in 1890: the egg cream, which used Grade A milk or *echt* cream (Yiddish and Dutch for "real" cream), chocolate syrup and seltzer. Queens is also famous for its dairies, including Queensboro, Dairylea and the Elmhurst Dairy, Inc., which was founded in 1919 and is still based in Jamaica, Queens.

Baby Ruth and Butterfinger Candies

Another sign that is hiding behind a tall, modern, multistory high-rise building that was recently built on Delancey Street is this delectable morsel of an ad, which is the second ad I captured after Omega Oil. This beauty of a sign gave me so much momentum and was also recommended by Vincenzo, my partner, who found many of these images while riding his construction van through New York City. Needing an eye-level shot for this, I talked the manager of the now disappeared five-and-dime department store to let me get on the roof. Sadly, four years later, this campaign would have been much more difficult to photograph due to world events that changed the lives of New Yorkers and people around the world forever. But part of the wonder of exploring my urban landscape was the adventures of getting access to an interior to get

Baby Ruth Candy & Butterfinger—Delancey Street, New York City. Taken March 1997. Ad circa 1930. Hung in NYHS Exhibition.

to an exterior of a building. For weeks before this ad was finally re-obscured, the building in front had been dug to its foundation, and the Butterfinger ad was finally visible by street passersby once again for a brief hungry bite.

In a phone call with Nestlé, which then had the patent for this early twentieth-century candy bar, its historian shared some tidbits about the bar. I learned that Baby Ruth was developed in 1921 and named after President Grover Cleveland's daughter, who died at the age of twelve.

Curtis's Candy of Chicago (1921–64) sold Baby Ruth to Standard Brands when it dissolved and was then bought by Nabisco. The Nestlé Food Corporation finally acquired the candy bar in 1990. The Nestlé historian deduced that the ad must have been painted in 1930, since after the stock market crash, Curtis's stopped its advertising for a number of years. Butterfinger Candy was another invention of the Curtis's Candy Company of Chicago, Illinois, in 1923, with the name being chosen by a public contest. Company

founder Otto Schnering had both Butterfinger and Baby Ruth bars dropped out of planes in the days before the stock market crash of 1929, which helped them gain their wide appeal.[65]

Still a Halloween favorite in the tiny bite-size wrapped version, Baby Ruth candy has staying power. The sign still dwells in the shadows of a modern structure, no longer able to watch the frantic Williamsburg Bridge traffic or candy being dropped from the sky.

PLANTERS PEANUTS

This is another dubious vintage mural of which I've questioned its veracity. The sign faces the rising sun and would surely have been much more faded if it were indeed authentic.

Kevin Walsh wrote me this e-mail in 1999 in response to my posting this image on the campaign website: "Hey, we've both been taken in by that Planters Peanuts ad in Ridgewood. A few days ago I got the news that that ad was painted in 1985 when they

were filming *Brighton Beach Memoirs*…I may have to start a page with amazing re-creations, since I have three of them now."[66] Walsh writes this on his site about this sign:

Planters Peanuts Always Fresh! Your friendly Planters Peanuts salesman, along with the ever-present Mr. Peanut, has been preaching the gospel of nuts from the Seneca Avenue elevated platform in Ridgewood since at least the

1930s, and possibly before that. At least I thought it did. I've been informed that this ad has only been there since 1985, when the Seneca Avenue station appeared in the movie Brighton Beach Memoirs! *It's so realistic, it has me completely fooled. Note the grinding/repairing and typewriter and cutlery ads above the Planters ad—those are apparently real. Other Forgotten Fans have told me that a Planters' ad was indeed*

Planters Peanuts—Ridgewood, Queens. Taken August 1997. Ad's authenticity in question.

on this site before the movie was shot. So for me, this ad is shrouded in mystery.[67]

Honestly, I don't think the signs above the ad are authentic either. Compared to other Planters Peanuts signs I've photographed, like the ones in Wilkes-Barre, Pennsylvania, where the brand originates, this Mr. Peanut figure isn't really a good likeness (see Missing Mr. Peanut in Wilkes-Barre,

Pennsylvania).[68] The original Mr. Peanut was tall, with lanky legs.

On one of our fading ad tours through Scranton and Wilkes-Barre, we came across the original building where Italian immigrant Amedeo Obici built his peanut empire. Obici and his brother-in-law Mario Peruzzi founded the unincorporated Planters Peanuts & Chocolate Company in Wilkes-Barre, Pennsylvania, in 1906. According

to the Planters Peanuts website, a grade-school artist, Antonio Gentile, submitted his sketch of Mr. Peanut and won a brand icon contest. A commercial graphic artist later added a top hat, monocle and cane. A three-story image of Mr. Peanut was painted on the side of the original factory on the Main Street entrance, with another large Mr. Peanut painted on the back facing the Lackawanna Railroad line. Mr. Peanut stood tall, watching the trains pass for decades until, in 2006, on the 100th anniversary of the company's founding, Mr. Peanut had a catastrophic encounter with progress and a wrecker's ball.

In August 2006, several organizations in the Wilkes-Barre area that knew of the plans of local developer Marvin Slomowitz to demolish this historical landmark and build a forty-thousand-square-foot strip mall tried to save the building from destruction. Thom Greco, a local businessman who, according to Denise Allabaugh of the *Citizen's Voice*, "owns a plethora of Planters' memorabilia," led a campaign with the help of a local radio DJ named Jenn to sell "Save Mr. Peanut" wristbands for $5 each. Allabaugh also reported that Greco hoped the $1,200 raised by his campaign might be used to ensure the proper preservation of the building's grand façade, which was agreed upon to remain.

An appeal by the Young Professionals Association of Northeast Pennsylvania, in which my photos of Mr. Peanut were used to try to include the warehouse behind the building where the Mr. Peanut sign was painted and the adjacent wall to the façade where another Mr. Peanut sign was painted, also fell on deaf ears. According to the developer, the historic façade "encompasses the front of the building and did not apply to Mr. Peanut's picture on the side, according to the agreement."

Slomowitz categorized the warehouses with the signs as "anything but historical." According to Allabaugh, Wilkes-Barre city councilman Jim McCarthy, along with a crowd of supporters of preserving the warehouses on which these beautiful antique signs were painted, watched as the building where Mr. Peanut stood for half a century was demolished "with lumps in their throats."[69]

In Joni Mitchell's 1970 hit "Big Yellow Taxi," she croons how they "paved paradise and put up a parking lot." Sometimes instead of a parking lot, they put up a strip mall. I have yet to visit this strip mall. I miss my visits to Mr. Peanut. "Don't it always seem to go that you don't know what you've got till it's gone?"

UNEEDA BISCUIT

In 1997, I spoke with a Nabisco historian who asserted that Uneeda Biscuit was introduced in 1898 and was the first product to bear the name of the National Biscuit Company, later known as Nabisco Foods. That same year, according to *Advertising Age dot com*, the Philadelphia advertising agency N. W. Ayer & Son launched the first prepackaged biscuit, Uneeda, with the slogan "Lest you forget, we say it yet, Uneeda Biscuit." Nabisco went on to launch the first million-dollar advertising campaign for Uneeda.[70] Due to the proliferation of remnant Uneeda Biscuit ads nationwide (the French Quarter in New Orleans has a famous one), it is evident that this painted sign was part of this million-dollar advertising budget that was allocated to outdoor advertising (also see page 212).

Uneeda Biscuit—Malcolm X Boulevard (formerly Reid Avenue), Brooklyn. Taken July 1998. Ad circa 1905. Hung in NYHS Exhibition.

GOLD MEDAL FLOUR

Gold Medal Flour ads are up there with Fletcher's Castoria ads for staying power, as the grades of lead paint used allowed them to weather so well. You can make out above the Gold Medal logo and to the right of a steel support rivet the names Washburn-Crosby—an 1877 partnership between the flour's founder, Cadwallader C. Washburn, and John Crosby. After a flour dust explosion that destroyed the old Minneapolis mill, a new one was built and was the first in the world to use automatic steel rollers. By 1907, Washburn & Crosby launched its long-running advertising slogan, "Eventually…Why not now?" According to the Gold Medal Flour website:

B.S. Bull, the company's advertising manager, is credited with the creation of the slogan. As the story goes, he was editing a wordy text about the superior quality of Gold Medal Flour and found, that when he was finished he had edited out all the words except 4: "Eventually." He then added, "Why Not Now?"

Gold Medal Flour—Ferry Terminal, Staten Island. Taken August 1998. Ad circa 1910.

Having had this brilliant idea, he was struck with self-doubt and tossed the paper into the wastebasket. It was said to have been found by a young member of the firm, James Ford Bell, who later became the first president of General Mills, Inc. (The slogan was used on billboards, company trucks, train cars, flour bags and in the company's printed advertisements, appearing as late as the early 1950's. Other companies adopted the slogan as their own; it was seen in political cartoons; the slogan was the title for a Sunday sermon; and it even appeared as the front-page headline of the Cincinnati Times-Star *with a small-print notation, "With apologies to Gold Medal Flour.")[71]*

According to the Chicago Advertising Federation website, in 1921,

a Gold Medal Flour ad created by the agency, Blackett-Sample-McFarland, developed a picture puzzle with answers so obvious the company was flooded with mail from consumers. To answer the letters, company officials thought it would be best to respond with a letter signed by a woman. The character, Betty Crocker, was created with a signature only. By 1940 Betty Crocker was the second best known woman in America, running only behind Eleanor Roosevelt.[72]

Unfortunately, Staten Island has never been a good source of fading ads. Compared to Queens, which still sports more than a handful of beauties, this is the only ad to represent this borough. But it is one heck of a sign. I will need to scour the borough of Richmond carefully with Kevin Walsh and his crew again someday soon I hope. Eventually...Why not now?[73]

CADET DOG FOOD

Pet owners take pet food for granted. Most people think prepared pet foods have been around since canned baked beans, but the invention of the kibble and dried chunks (or extruded food pellets) and canned moist morsels we feed to our dogs isn't quite half a century old. An organic pet food retail website provided the following historical context:

Before the advent of pet foods, most dogs and cats lived off of grains, meats, table scraps and homemade food from their owners. It wasn't until the mid-1800's that the world saw its first food made specifically for dogs. An American electrician, James Spratt concocted the first dog treat. Living in London at the time, he witnessed dogs around a ship yard eating scraps of discarded biscuits. A light bulb went off in his head and shortly thereafter he introduced his dog food, made up of wheat meals, vegetables and meat. His company flourished and by 1890 he was taken over by a large corporation and production had begun in the United States as well.

Cadet Dog Food—Third Avenue, Brooklyn. Taken November 1998. Ad circa 1950.

But it wasn't until the early 1900's that pet food really caught on. Canned horse meat was introduced in the United States under the Ken-L-Ration brand after WWI as a means to dispose of deceased horses. The 1930's saw the introduction of canned cat food and dry meat-meal dog food by the Gaines Food Co. During WWII metal used for cans was set aside for the war effort, which nearly ruined the canned pet food industry. But by the time WWII ended, pet food was off and running again, and sales had reached $200 million…At first, canned pet food was the primary type sold, but by 1956 the first extruded pet foods were hitting store shelves. Extrusion is the process by which pet foods are formed into pellets, and then sprayed with synthetic nutrients to compensate for nutrition lost during processing.[74]

According to the Pet Food Institute, pet food companies flourished even during the lean years of the early twentieth century. On its website it claims the following:

The Depression of the '30's may have meant hard times for industry, but the merchandising of dog food germinated and spread countrywide. One report accounted for 221 brands of canned dog food with about 200 of this total produced at a half dozen canning plants. The plants did the canning; the merchandisers supplied labels. The situation was similar with dry pet foods. All that was needed was a brand name and empty bags.

Working capital was minimal and the market wide open. Metropolitan New York saw Cadet brand canned ration (Re-Dan Packing Co.) and Snappy canned dog food (Foster Canning Co.) as the two leading sellers.[75]

Daniel Pearlstein was the owner of Cadet Dog Food and Re-Dan Packing. I learned this from comments from his granddaughter Leslie Sanders Axelrod on the *Fading Ad* Blog, where she was reunited with a cousin with whom she used to spend holidays at their home in Rego Park, Queens. I posted pictures Richard Boll had sent me of a Cadet Ad that was briefly exposed on the wooden slats of a house in Maspeth, Queens.[76] It was from this ad we learned that one of the ingredients of Cadet Dog Food was "chlorophyllin." I imagine this additive was to promote better dog breath. The Cadet Dog Food image pictured here was from a painted ad on Third Avenue in Boerum Hill, Brooklyn, not far from the terminus of the Gowanus Canal. The building on which it was painted has since been demolished, and a new high-rise will soon be in its place.

A Coke
and a
Smoke

COCA-COLA AND MECCA SMOKES PENTIMENTO

In explaining a layered fading ad, I've always used the term *pentimento*, a painterly term that describes evidence of a previous work on a canvas seen through an existing upper layer. Viewing these works under varied wavelengths of light, like ultraviolet, infrared and even X-ray scanning, can aid scientists in deciphering both palimpsests and pentimenti. The use of the word pentimento in "street and photography" has also been cited on the Internet as a term "used in a modern sense to describe the appearance of the sides of buildings with painted advertising." Often when newer ads are painted over older ads, "the paint wears away to reveal the older layers." Examples of this can be seen in the work I did in the Netherlands in 1998 while photographing fading ads in Amsterdam.[77]

In the last fifteen years that I've been documenting vintage advertising on brick, I still get exhilarated when I find a Coca-Cola ad. It doesn't matter how faded, or how skillfully or sometimes not so skillfully painted, this graphic mark transcends time—this is a logo for the ages. Not only is it the most popular soft drink in the world, it is also one of the most often found remnants of the early twentieth-century outdoor advertising campaigns. Here is a description of the product and trademark taken from the *Logo Blog*:

Originally [it was] *intended as a "patent medicine" when it was invented in the late 19th century by pharmacist John S. Pemberton as a "coca wine." Coca-Cola has dominated the worldwide soft drink market for decades now. The Coca-Cola logo, like the product itself, is rated among the most recognized logo design and brands in the world. The first Coca-Cola logo was created*

form of formal handwriting in the United States during that period. The red and white colored scheme in the Coca-Cola logo was kept simple and distinctive to lure young minds. Even the Coca-Cola bottle symbolized the "youthful exuberance of America." Since then, various designs of the Coca-Cola bottle had been released over the decades. But the ever popular version is the famous 1915's curved-vessel bottle called the "contour bottle," better known to many as the "hobble skirt" bottle. Though mistakenly designed as cacao pod, the bottle like Coca-Cola logo has been highly popular and is often regarded as the best design ever. The Coca-Cola logo was first advertised in the Atlanta Journal *in 1915 and also appeared on the display of Pemberton's pharmacy. A Coca-Cola dispenser with the popular logo design was later created by Raymond Loewy. The Coca-Cola logo got registered as a trademark in 1887 and has since then become the brand's corporate identity.*[78]

by John Pemberton's partner and bookkeeper, Frank Mason Robinson, in 1885. Thinking that the two Cs would look well in advertising, it was Robinson who came up with the name and chose the logo's distinctive cursive script.

The typeface used, known as Spencerian script, was developed in the mid 19th century and was the dominant

Almost imperceptibly overlaying this Coke ad was perhaps the oldest Mecca

Cigarettes ad in New York City. From the price of five cents, and from a similar sign on the East Side (page 90), I can date this sign between 1910 and 1912. When I first glanced at this sign on the corner of Carmine and Bleecker Streets in Greenwich Village where Sixth Avenue also intersects, I could vaguely make out the distinctive Coca-Cola logo, but the Mecca Cigarettes ad was still a mystery. The building wall faced south, explaining the intensely faded aspect of this pentimento. I had to get on the roof to take this. The pizza joint downstairs did not have access to the roof. So I went next door and rang the bell. "Who is there?" "Photographer!" I got buzzed in. The woman who lived there had roof access, but we had to move her refrigerator away from the staircase to the roof that was being blocked. I was amazed that she let a total stranger do all this to get on her roof with a camera. Once I was up there, I could clearly see the pack of ten unfiltered cigarettes open for the taking.

In the course of documenting these signs, I have become aware of the profound specificity within certain niches of advertising enthusiasm. There are people who only collect Coca-Cola ads. There are the breweriana fans. Tobaccoiana fans are a breed of their own. Given that there was so much outdoor advertising in the sale of tobacco products (Mail Pouch and Owl Cigars, just to name two), there surely are still thousands of remnants scattered across the globe. An even more specific fan base is the enthusiasts of the colorful card collectibles that were generated from the nicotine ad campaigns. James A. Shaw offers his insight about Mecca Cigarettes on his colorful and comprehensive website:

The centuries-old city of Mecca is nestled among the ancient hills of Arabia. Mecca was the birthplace of the prophet Muhammad, and has been the destination of millions of Moslem pilgrims. Mecca Cigarettes was named after this holy city when introduced by the Kinney Bros. Tobacco Company in 1878. Mecca sales benefited from a heavy dose of advertising dollars following the dissolution of The American Tobacco Company trust in 1911. Magazine and newspaper ads, a wood framed sign, plus several sets of attractive cigarette insert cards boosted consumer awareness. Ads published in 1915 claimed Mecca "the largest selling brand in America today." America's fascination with the mystic of the Mideast would last until the First World War. When Turkey allied itself with the enemies of the United States, plus the 1913 introduction of the modern "American Blend" Camel cigarette, the popularity of the different Turkish and Egyptian brands plummeted. Even though the Turkish brands would no longer play an important role with smokers, exotic Turkish tobacco would continue to be imported and used as a "seasoning" in the Camel, Lucky Strike, and Chesterfield brands.[79]

Bronx Coca-Cola

(*pages 82–83*)

If I recall correctly, I distinctly remember scaling the wall of this subway platform with the help of Vincenzo to take this shot.

The following is from Kevin Walsh's website:

Thanks to the MTA's renovations of several stations along the White Plain's Road line in the Bronx, this sign can now be seen in its full magnificence. Before renovation this sign could only be seen from the

catwalk on the west side of the elevated structure just south of the station's platform or from the street. Taken from the #2 terminus at 241st Street & White Plains Road. Wakefield, The Bronx.[80]

Philip Morris

The *New York Times* quoted me in 1998 as calling these signs "tombstones." Although I was taken out of context (I see most of these signs as signs of life, metaphors for survival), this particular sign does have a tombstone quality. In retrospect, the ghostly image of the World Trade Center in the distance is indeed haunting.

As a child, I enjoyed watching cigarette commercials, the music always drawing me in. My love affair with cigarette commercials started with the Marlboro theme, so *Bonanza*-like in its bravado. The Marlboro man

was pretty hot, too. Later, I was hooked on the Benson & Hedges theme that was performed by a Tijuana Brass sound-alike (and album cover look-alike) group called the Brass Ring. The song was entitled "The Disadvantages of You," and I actually went out and bought the single in 1967.[81] I played it constantly and danced around my room with an imaginary cigarette that, of course, was "a silly millimeter longer" than the other brands, so I often got my imaginary cigarette caught up my nose or slammed in my bathroom door by accident, just like in the

commercials. I also remember loving the ironic title; within the context of the cigarette commercial, the disadvantage was meant to be the clumsy length of the cigarette, not the fact that smoking the cigarette actually killed you. Fortunately for me, I got hooked on TV commercial music and not the product it was selling. Philip Morris owns both cigarette brands Marlboro and Benson & Hedges.

In the United States, Benson & Hedges was acquired by Philip Morris in 1953, when "the boards of directors of Benson &

Hedges and Philip Morris agreed to a merger of the two firms."[82] Today, Philip Morris (strategically rebranded as Altria Group in 2003) is the largest shareholder of familiar American food brands such as Kraft (which merged with General Foods), Nabisco and an exhaustive list of popular cigarette brands and wineries worldwide.[83]

Reporter for *Time* magazine Randy James stated, "The first tobacco advertisement in the United States ran in 1789 when what is now the Lorillard Tobacco Company promoted their snuff in a local New York newspaper."[84] In this article, James goes on further to explain the dramatic increase of the use of tobacco products in the United States due to advertising:

By the late 19th century, two innovations had helped launch cigarette companies to national prominence. The first, a cigarette-making machine introduced in the 1880s, dramatically increased production; instead of producing some 40,000 hand-rolled cigarettes a day, a company with one of these machines could produce 4 million cigarettes daily. The second development came in the late 1870s with the invention of color lithography, which revolutionized advertising and packaging and helped developing brands strengthen their identities. Using this new technology, companies began including small cigarette cards in every box as premiums. These collectible trading cards depicted movie stars, famous athletes and even Native American chiefs.[85]

In 1964, the U.S. surgeon general warnings on cigarettes were introduced. Cigarette commercials were totally banned from television in the United States in the early 1970s. According to the World Health Organization (which wants a ban on all tobacco advertising), there are an estimated 1.3 billion cigarette smokers worldwide. Of these smokers, 33 to 50 percent will be killed by their habit.[86] By the end of the twenty-first century, if smoking trends continue, 1 billion people will die due to smoking-related illnesses. This is not including deaths caused by secondhand smoke. I can think of safer, more enjoyable ways of controlling the planet's exponential growth in population, can't you?

OPPOSITE
Philip Morris—Fifth Avenue and East 20th Street. Taken June 1998. Ad circa 1940s.

GOLD MEDAL FLOUR/ MECCA SMOKES EAST SIDE PENTIMENTO

Another great pentimento with nature doing her tricks!

MECCA SMOKES EAST SIDE

Persistent Satisfaction.

Today that means "insistent addiction."

Gold Medal Flour/Mecca Smokes pentimento—East 70th Street and York Avenue, New York City. Taken June 1997. Ad circa 1910.

Mecca Smokes—East 70th Street and York Avenue, New York City. Taken June 1997. Ad circa 1910.

SoHo Coca-Cola

The translucent "water tower" on the left is a sculpture by Rachel Whiteread. It is a resin cast of the interior of an actual water tower. In a 2001 piece called *Chronology*, Mickey Stretton compares my work with Whiteread's while formulating the following theory about the exploration of time as a fourth dimension in visual arts:

I also have a great fascination for Installation art, such as that of Rachel Whiteread. Whiteread creates sculpture of casts from negative space that the object occupies, and the spatial language she uses is another great example of looking closer at something to see beyond the expected. Had I a tin-opener close by (not to mention a few extra pages) I would probably open a whole can of worms about using space as a method of communication. I haven't though, so I won't. Besides, the whole issue of time is much more interesting and so with time in mind, I'll move swiftly on.

Before I can talk about the works of artists whose use of time I find inspirational and thought-provoking, I guess I must first try to describe what I find so intriguing about the concept of time itself. Whilst I don't let myself lose sleep over it, the whole concept of time poses so many unanswerable questions that I find completely fascinating. How do we understand the notion of time, when we can't see or feel it? Why does a minute go faster when you're having fun than when you're waiting for a bus? Is time elastic, able to be stretched or otherwise manipulated? What relationships exist between space and time?

Apologies if you think that last bit got a bit heavy, but stick with me and I'll see if I can explain what I mean. Of any roll of film to come out of my camera, at least four or five shots will invariably be of rusting signs, derelict shop frontages or similar urban typography, so when a friend introduced me to the work of Frank Jump I felt an immediate empathy.

Jump is a photographer whose work (www.frankjump.com) concentrates on the ageing ads painted onto the sides of factories or shops around his native city of New York, and reveals a shared preoccupation and fascination with found imagery, typography and urban architecture.

But more than that, the work also relies inherently on the influence of time, and as such provokes thought and begs the question: what story do they tell about the building/advert/product? Is it art or is it graphic design, but these pieces are often selling products that are no longer on sale and are complete strangers to today's world of commercialism, so surely they must be art? If they are art, how much of their beauty is a result of their age? What did they look like a year ago? A decade or a century ago? Would they have been considered beautiful then?

Jump isn't attempting to answer these questions, but instead just trying to get the viewer to ask themselves the questions it provokes. A

couple of paragraphs ago I proposed the question "How do we understand the notion of time, when we can't see it or feel it?" In this case we can visualize time by its effects on the ageing sign, but we can't see time itself—only a vehicle or language that visually represents it. Of course, you could argue that a clock is an adequate way to see time, but even then we are using numbers, in standard measurements of hours, minutes and seconds,

as a means to visualize it. And besides, how accurate is a clock as a way of seeing time (they run fast or slow, or stop completely—time never stops, does it?).[87]

Which leads me to postulate that progress, like time, never stops—or does it? In this photograph, Duckett & Adler is still visible, as is Wintergarden. Although partly responsible for its partial demise, the Colossal Media outdoor advertising company has been using a

fraction of this wall for new advertising. As in the Liberty Beer sign (page 97), there is the ambivalence of having a perfect fade interrupted, even in the name of progress. Thus is the cycle of the urban landscape continuing in its dynamistic unfolding—a collage of commercial artistic endeavors building layer upon layer for future fading.

OPPOSITE
SoHo Coca-Cola—Grand Street facing West Broadway, New York City. Taken September 1998. Ad circa 1910.

Breweriana

Liberty Beer

In my search of breweriana sites of trays and other ephemera, I found a tray with the name "Liberty Beer American Brewing Co. Rochester NY."[88] This site also gives a timeline for this Rochester brewery, and the date range of 1889–1920 seems to be when this ad was executed. During Prohibition, the company changed its name to Rochester Food Products Company. Rochester, New York, is on the Genesee River and has the magnificent High Falls adorning its waterfront before it empties into Lake Ontario.[89]

Shortly after the Iroquois tribes were forced out of this area, Colonel Nathaniel Rochester founded the town in 1803. Rochester is nicknamed the "Flour City," but it easily could have been nicknamed the "Brew City." According to Rochester city historian Ruth Rosenberg-Naperstack,

"The earliest documented distillery opened in Rochester in 1815."[90] According to Rosenberg-Naperstack:

Intoxication was a social problem that arrived along with the earliest settlers; an individual lifestyle carried from communities left behind. Distilleries were among the earliest industries in the Genesee country. Farmers grew corn and rye for sale to distilleries because the profits were higher than wheat sales to flour mills. A jug of hard liquor was commonly passed when a roof was raised or a field of wheat was cut by community effort.

Taverns were among the earliest businesses built, finding ready use among travelers moving into the new country. It became a friendly gathering place for the men to tell stories of the Revolution, of wild animals and adventures.

Excessive drinking was not unnoticed, but it took decades for the attitudes towards drinking and hospitality to evolve. The liquor jug was considered indispensable when dozens of men gathered to raise a roof and running a distillery in the days when liquor was perceived as medicinal was not frowned upon.[91]

Rosenberg-Naperstack stated that there were many mergers and partnerships of breweries in the nineteenth century. The German population in 1812 was scarce, but by what was called the 1848 German Revolution,

PREVIOUS PAGES
Guinness Beer—Long Island City, Queens. Taken September 1997. Ad circa 1960s.

OPPOSITE
Liberty Beer—Canal and Lafayette Streets, Chinatown, New York City. Taken August 1998. Ad circa 1910.

thousands of Germans had immigrated to Rochester. This explains the many types of German city brews found in this ad. "Culmbacher" was most likely "Kulmbacher." The American Brewing Company evolved from a partnership between Meyer and Loebs (1861) and then was renamed the Lion Brewing Company (1879) and was bought out by the Loebs Brothers in 1885 before finally being incorporated as the American Brewing Company in 1889. Rosenberg–Naperstack goes on further to say that before stopping production in 1950, "In its heyday in 1890 the American Brewing Company on Hudson near Drayton Street covered a full block with its fireproof six-story brick building."[92]

Rosenberg–Naperstack also claims that the temperance movement started in 1827 by the Rochester Presbytery.[93] Thus the brewing and distillery industry and the temperance movement in Rochester grew hand in hand. Rochester was home to many forward thinkers. This socially influential list includes temperance and women's rights pioneer Susan B. Anthony, abolitionist Frederick Douglass and anarchist Emma Goldman, just to name a few. This jewel of a boomtown was also the home of Kodak, a company that profoundly altered the course of the use of the photographic image in media and social communications. A bulk of my photographic archive was documented using Kodak products.[94]

The Liberty Beer sign was uncovered in the summer of 1998. Previously, it had remained peering over handbag hawkers and Excellent Dumpling eaters at the intersection of Lafayette and Canal Streets for thirteen years until it was finally covered by a new T-Mobile ad, commissioned to the Colossal Media outdoor advertising company. Colossal Media is known for its slick, hand-painted ads, often done in the style of the early twentieth-century billboards. Here is an excerpt from a letter I wrote to the Landmarks Preservation Commission on behalf of Colossal in December 2007 in support of its efforts to gain the airspace rights to a building in SoHo with a vintage Coca-Cola ad (page 92):

Colossal Media produces modern ads that are visually exciting—ads that will become tomorrow's classic fading ads. With the hand-painted brickface ad medium, Colossal Media is continuing the tradition of the painted ad that has become an indelible symbol of New York's urban landscape. Tourists come to New York, the mecca for world commerce—and expect to see both the historic and modern—the old classic and the new classic. Sign enthusiasts all over the world,

like Sam Roberts UK Brick Ads Blog[95] marvel over Colossal's painted mural ads, which have become a tourist attraction. No one expects fading ads to last forever. Just like fashion trends, they come and go. I'd rather see a vintage ad covered by a classic Colossal modern work of art than with one of those crass outdoor illuminated billboards or a dingy nylon fabric hung ad. The pride Colossal Media takes in their work is evident in their finished product.

There really is a lot going on in this image, even the MetLife blimp peeking through on the left of the sign. From what I can extract using my Photoshop "Hue/Saturation Centrifuge," the wording across the top seems to spell "Hollenbeck Company," with the body of the text stating, "Importers and Bottlers of Beer—Imported Pilsener, Humbser, Kaiser, Munchener, Culmbacher, and Warsteiner Beers." To the upper left of the script written "Liberty" is the name "Rochester." I'm quite ambivalent about seeing this sign covered, as much as I am all for progress.

GUINNESS BEER

I believe these images are on what was the Guinness brewery in Long Island City (pages 94–95). The intent of painting this sign was so commuters on the Long Island Rail Road and drivers on the Long Island Expressway would see it, where it is still clearly visible. The following history was provided on a Guinness beer enthusiast's website:

In 1934, long time Irish bottler of Guinness Stout (and US importer of Guinness, Bass Ale and Perrier water), E.&J. Burke, Ltd., opened a brewery in Long Island City (Queens), NY. They brewed and marketed their own Burke's Beer, Ale and Stout and, as war in Europe loomed in the late '30's, Guinness and Burke began discussions about brewing Guinness in the Burke facility for the US market.

In 1943, Guinness bought the Burke brewery from the failing Burke and in 1948 began brewing Guinness Extra Stout for the US market. It was only the second

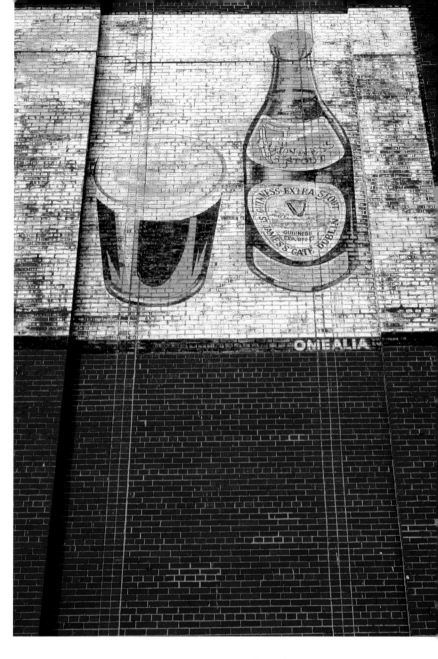

Guinness Beer close-up.

brewery Guinness would run outside of Ireland. (The first being the long-lived UK Park Royal brewery in London which closed in 2005). The Long Island City brewery closed in 1954.[96]

City of Immigrants and the Mack Sign Company

As apparitional as sails that cross
Some page of figures to be filed away
—Hart Crane, "To Brooklyn Bridge"

New York's faded vintage signs constitute an important element in the city's business history. They remind us pointedly that the New York of an earlier time was a city of industry and business. It was a city of manufacturing, Whitman's lusty place of work and sweat. The "Manhatta" of Paul Strand and Charles Sheeler. A city that puffed smoke. It was also a city of immigrants. Many of the surviving signs bear the names of people born in Russia, Germany, Italy, Switzerland. Almost incredibly, these men (and some women) left their names on the walls we walk beneath today. They were little men, obscure figures. They lived in tenements downtown on the East Side, in Brooklyn, Harlem or the Bronx. They went to work. They left their names behind.

The stories were as varied as life itself. There is Harriet Hubbard Ayer, who abandoned her life as a wealthy society matron to found a cosmetics company that manufactured facial cream and later became the highest-paid woman journalist in America. Many were successful businessmen who retired into wealth and security. They received obituaries in the *New York Times* and were cited for their many philanthropies and benefits

to mankind. Such were, for instance, Sol Mutterperl (popular-priced ladies' handbags), who endowed scholarships at the Jewish Theological Seminary; Samuel Rubel (coal and ice), who entertained more than ten thousand orphans at his expense at Coney Island; Benjamin Lowenstein (Nassau Smelting & Refining), for whom a students' lounge at Columbia University was named; Louis Friedman (Friedman & Herskovitz, Furriers), "active in the affairs of the Hebrew National Orphans Home"; Israel Cummings, president of the Alumni Association of the Education Alliance, part of the Federation of Jewish Philanthropies; Louis Philippe, "a pioneer in the development of indelible lipstick"; William Olden (Olden Camera), identified with Jewish philanthropic and communal activities; Harry Shulman (Baker Brush Co.), who received a special citation from the United Jewish Appeal in recognition of his philanthropic work; and Max Berley (Berley Real Estate), who was treasurer of the University Settlement House. Other prominent figures include Charles B. Sheridan, who made ninety-one trips to Europe, and Hamilton Disbrow, who was known as the "dean of commuters" of the

Delaware, Lackawanna & Western Railroad, having traveled almost daily to New York from his home in New Jersey on this line for more than seventy years.

Others were active in politics, like James J. Riordan (Mohahan Express), who was an officer in the election campaigns of James J. Walker (New York City mayor) and Al Smith (New York State governor); Otto Shulhof (American Neon Light & Sign Corp.), who numbered among his friends "former Governor Smith, former Mayor James J. Walker, Postmaster General James A. Farley and Senator Robert F. Wagner"; and Ernest F. Eilert (Eilert Printing), who ran for borough president in Manhattan in 1921.

Many were family businesses that went through several generations, such as the three generations of Richard A. Bachia who made fine Havana cigars; the three generations of the Trischett family engaged in bias bindings; and the three (or more) generations of the Gross family of S.G. Gross, pawnbrokers.

There are tragic stories also, like William Klatzco, who committed suicide by inhaling illuminating gas in his office at 105 East 29th Street; and Hyman A. Posner, who swallowed poison while on the "Jungle Walk" at the Bronx Zoo. He left a note: "I have lost my nerve and pep because business has been so bad." Moses Gootman was murdered in his home in the middle of the night by an intruder. Louis Reiff committed suicide by throwing himself from a window at the New Yorker Hotel on New Year's Eve.

The importance of New York's vintage signs is particularly pertinent to the period 1900 to 1930, when the painted wall sign was used extensively to advertise products and business locations. These signs were a primary medium of the time, and thousands have survived (past their time) into the twenty-first century. In midtown New York, they cluster heavily in the garment area, where a single wall will often have a dozen or more individual signs. They were furriers, manufacturers of cloaks (coats), suits, underwear, waists (blouses), dresses, skirts, raincoats, neckwear, hats, embroidery, leather goods, knitwear, silk and cotton goods. They manufactured cigars, toys and bedding. There are signs for restaurants, pawnbrokers, hotels, banks, moving companies, commission merchants, import and export companies, butchers, paper and twine dealers…You name it, we got it! In more recent times, these are the yimin, the leftover men of Yuan, China.

I bought my first 35mm camera in March 1986 and took a picture of my first wall sign on April 19, 1986. This was a sign overlooking the Holland Tunnel exit near the corner of Varick and Canal Streets. For many years, I called this sign the "Hot Cow." It showed a cow with the letters HOT and the rest erased. Years later, Frank Florianz sent me a photo of the sign in its original state. It was an advertisement for Hotel Bar Butter. It was painted out totally many years ago. Many others from that early period are no longer with us. Some early favorites were Charles Hellmuth Printing Ink on West 18th Street, Chelsea Warehouses on Broadway near 125th Street, Dinoto's Bread near Yankee Stadium, the Penn View Hotel on West 34th Street, Admiration Cigars/Bowery Dept. Store on the Bowery near Canal Street and Hartz Mountain (altered to Art Mountain) on Cooper Square.

Fleeting phenomena of the rainbow. We grab our cameras and run to get the photo before it fades…

To Frank Jump, these signs are the symbols of our own human frailty, our very temporary presence in a life that ends in death. I first heard of Frank in 1998, when he exhibited photos at the New-York Historical Society. I was not able to attend the opening but saw the show later, managed to get his telephone number, talked with him about our mutual interest and then sent him a book (by a German author) that showed an earlier artist's interest in the wall sign. (We were not the first.) Several years later, I met Frank when he had an exhibition at the Williamsburg Art & Historical Center. I remember he was very personable, very likable. But out the window was an angle on the Williamsburg bridge, and all I could really think about was how to get a photo of that. (Photographers are a funny lot and seldom very sociable.)

> But often when the laugh was loud,
> And highest gleamed the circling bowl,
> I saw what unseen passed the crowd,—
> The shadow on his soul.
> —Fitz-James O'Brien

About 2002, I put up a website devoted to signs in the Midtown Manhattan area from 14th to 42nd Streets. This drew the attention of a man named Bob Middleton, who had been the owner of the Mack Sign Company, commercial sign painters. Bob Middleton followed his father, Harry Middleton, in the business. In 1930, Harry Middleton bought the Mack Sign Company for seventy-five dollars from persons unknown, who were located in the Inwood section of Manhattan. Subsequently, Harry Middleton painted two of the most beautiful surviving signs in New York: Griffon Cutlery on West 19th Street and Necchi Sewing Machines on West 25th Street. His son, Bob Middleton, sent me material relating to the Mack Sign Company, such as layouts used by the painters when painting the signs. After much arm-twisting, I convinced Bob to write a description of how the work was done. This can be read on 14to42's Mack Sign page.[97] Recently, Bob was included in a documentary, *Up There*, directed by Malcolm Murray (2010). [Signs identifiably by the Mack Sign Company are noted in Frank Jump's collection of images.]

> *J'ai seul la clef de cette parade sauvage.*
> —*Rimbaud*

> *I alone have the key to this savage sideshow.*—*Varèse*

Walter Grutchfield, July 2011
14th to 42nd Street

Shoes,
Hats and
Assorted
Garments—
Wholesale
and Retail

UNITED THREAD MILLS

Manufacturers of sewing thread, cotton, nylon, synthetics.

According to Walter Grutchfield, Bob Middleton and Joseph Piscitelli of Mack Sign Company painted this sign in the period between 1965 and 1969. The United Thread Mills manufactured sewing thread in this textile mill at 146 Greene Street from 1962 to 1982. Originally located at 656 Broadway in 1942 for seven years, this company then moved to 54 Bleecker Street, where it remained from 1949 to 1962. In 1982, United Thread Mills moved from its Greene Street location to Rockville Centre, Long Island.[98]

This image appears as a city backdrop in Kubrick's *Eyes Wide Shut*, which was filmed in London but made to look like New York City. I've often wondered from where they lifted that image. The New York Landmarks Preservation Committee fought to have this sign left untouched but made a deal with an ad agency to only cover 15 percent of the visible ghost sign. You can see examples of this sign being painted over at "United Thread Mills in Transition" on the *Fading Ad Blog*.[99]

SEELY SHOULDER SHAPES

Incorporated from November 17, 1953, through December 15, 1959.

According to the *Manhattan Ghost Signs Digital Collection*,[100] an attractively designed new website created by Queens College graduates Otto Luna and Dana Rubin to catalogue the fading ads of the Garment District (using the extensive photo archive of Walter Grutchfield), Seely Shoulder Shapes was originally called Seely Shoulder Pad Corp., located at 263–5 West 40th Street from 1945 until 1956. Shoulder shapes or pads are still produced today for the fashion industry, but no longer at this address.

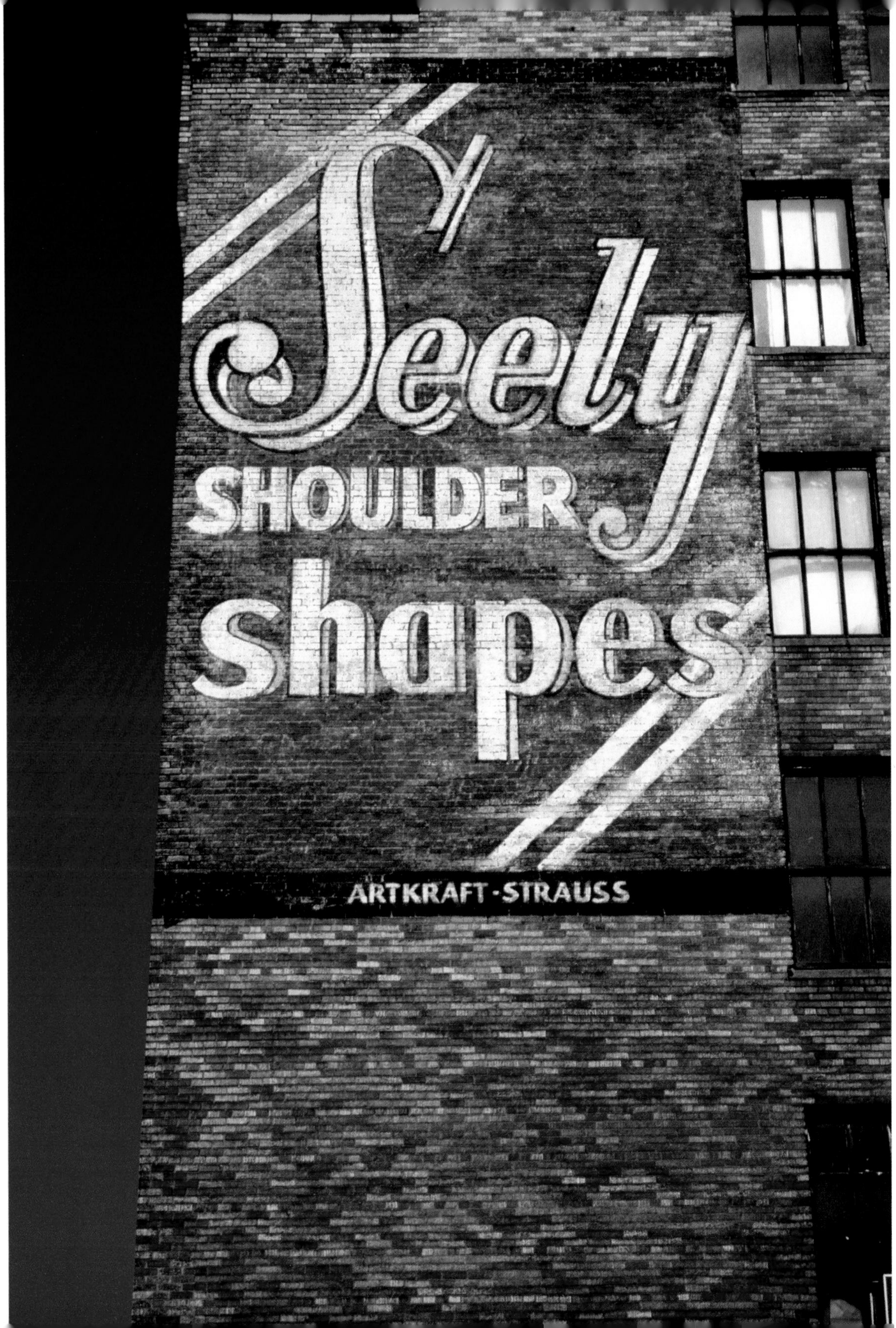
Seely
SHOULDER
shapes
ARTKRAFT-STRAUSS

In a *New York Times* article in which I was featured and provided the front-page image, David W. Dunlap stated the following about the fate of this sign: "Another vintage sign that is not destined to last much longer trumpets Seely Shoulder Shapes, a garment business from the 1950's. Painted by Artkraft Strauss, which is still in operation, the mural is at 265 West 40th Street, on the site where *The New York Times* is planning its new headquarters." After the New-York Historical Society show came down, I tried to sell the collection. One of my benefactors is the lovely Tama Starr, president of the Artkraft-Strauss outdoor advertising company,[101] whom I had the pleasure of spending an hour or more with, talking about the sign-painting industry. Starr was very encouraging of the campaign and gave me a copy of her seminal book about advertising, *Signs & Wonders: The Spectacular Marketing of America*.

In Starr's book, she speaks primarily on the illuminated sign industry, although she does touch on the origins of advertising and the innate ability of humans to create signs and symbols. In a section she calls "From Cave Artists to Wall Dogs," Starr addresses questions about which I've always speculated, like what was the first advertisement and who invented the wall ad? Starr writes:

The story of outdoor advertising traditionally begins with the first symbolic marketers, the cave dwellers during the Upper Paleolithic period, starting about 40,000 years ago. At Lascaux, France, and elsewhere, elaborate action murals depicting a variety of animals and lively hunting scenes portray the dynamic relationship between hunters and the migratory beasts who represented fundamental economic forces: food and clothing, the entire constellation of blessings that Nature could either bestow or withhold.

Anthropologists identify these Stone Age rendering— the first wall-mounted messages—as the earliest examples of both art and writing. They speculate that, like modern media, the messages were intended to influence as well as reflect the viewer's life. Like advertisements, they depict dreams fulfilled—the animals rushing into the hunters' traps—and urge specific, concrete action—Hunt! Be hunted!—on both parties to the economic transaction.

All known cultures use signs, in one form or another, to convey straightforward messages with immediacy. Anthropologist Ashley Montagu defines a sign as a "concrete denoter" with an inherent, specific meaning: "This is it; do something about it!" He points out the essentially human character of signs by noting that while many types of animals respond to signals—interruptions in an energy field for the purpose of communicating—only a few intelligent and highly trained animals can understand even the simplest signs.

History's first known poster bulletin was a notice of a reward for a runaway slave posted on a wall in the Egyptian city of Thebes more than 3,000 years ago. Egyptian merchants of the same periods chiseled sales messages into tall, square stone obelisks and roadside stone tablets called stelae, and painted them in bright colors to attract the attention of passersby.

In Pompeii, billboard-like walls covered with advertisements were preserved in the lava that engulfed them when Mount Vesuvius erupted in A.D. 79. Excavations there have revealed wall messages on the shady side of the marketplace too, offering enticing invitations along the lines of "For a Good Time, See Cora." And even earlier, in ancient Greece, innovative practitioners of what may arguably be the world's second-oldest profession (symbol-making being necessarily precedent) expanded their out-of-home client base by carving the message "ΕΠΟ☐ ΜΟΙ," "Follow Me," in the bottoms of their leather sandals,

leaving an impression in the clay pavement as well as in the imaginations of potential customers. The connection between the two ancient occupations was not limited to amateurs, however. Modern visitors to Kuşadasi in Turkey are shown magnificent Byzantine mosaics that once served as on-premises business signs for houses of pleasure.

The Romans brought the use of whitewashed walls with painted ads on them on their conquests throughout Europe. They also developed artful on-premise business signs specially designed for the illiterate, such as a friendly-looking bush denoting a tavern. Some ancient trade symbols—such

as the three golden balls of the pawnshop, the giant key of the locksmith, the big shoe of the shoemaker, and the red and white stripes of the barber— have remained in use for a thousand years and more.[102]

Tama Starr loved the image of Seely Shoulder Shapes and bought it. As I signed the photo for her, she signed her book for me:

Frank Jump! It's always a good sign to meet a new friend. Best wishes always, Tama Starr 7/14/00

I believe this image still hangs in Tama Starr's office.

CROWN COAT FRONTS

This collection of signs still overlooks the northeast corner of Union Square atop the New York Film Academy. I was fortunate enough to have been allowed on the roof by my friend Michael J. Young, who is now the provost, director of education at NYFA. Grutchfield provided

the following background information about the Crown Coat Front Company, as well as additional information gleaned from archival photographs:

Crown Coat Front was located at 105 E. 16 St. from 1947 to 1957/58. A coat front is defined by George E. Linton…

as "Trade term for a built-up stiffening or shape-retaining interlining for the fronts of coats, made of stitched layers of haircloth, felt and canvas." A few details have been lost and the color is considerably faded. Frank Jump has a nice photograph of Crown Coat Front and the Carl Fischer

Crown Coat Fronts—Union Square East, New York City. Taken April 1997. Ad circa 1950s.

Musical Instruments sign next to it on his website.

…An image dated 1933 on the New York Public Library's Digital Gallery[103] shows that prior to Crown Coat Front a sign painted in the same position read Hyman & Oppenheim / Human Hair Goods. Hyman & Oppenheim were longtime occupants of 105 E. 16ᵗʰ St. (from 1910 to 1931). The original

Hyman was Gerson Hyman (1852–1911), a native of Wirballen, Russian Poland (now Lithuania). His two sons, Louis Hyman (1882–?) and Joseph Hyman (1886–1932), succeeded him in the business. The original Oppenheim was Manuel Oppenheim (1851–1917). He was born in Neustadt, Suwalki province, also in Russian Poland (now Lithuania). He was in the

hair business with his brother, Heyne (or Heine) Oppenheim, in the 1870s before going into partnership with Gerson Hyman around 1885.

Manuel Oppenheim's son, Jesse Oppenheim (1876–1936), succeeded him in the business. When Jesse Oppenheim applied for a passport in 1920, a letter signed by Joseph Hyman was attached stating that

Oppenheim had at that time been with the corporation 27 years…Around 1939 Hyman & Oppenheim changed its name to Hyman & Hyman, and they were located at 38 W. 48th St… The business had also changed and seems to have dealt mostly in distribution of beauty products rather than strictly hair goods. Hyman & Hyman were in business until the early 1970s.[104]

To the far right of the Crown Coat Front Company Inc., MFGR'S (Manufacturers) of Civilian & Military Coat Fronts, it says "Carl Fischer Musical Instruments," which according to the New York Department of State, Division of Corporations, was incorporated on September 20, 1971, and dissolved on April 13, 1987. Carl Fischer Music Publishing was incorporated on July 31, 1923, and is still active.

Underneath that, it says "York Band Instruments Company Est. 1892." Below that it reads what I believe says "Mogi, Momomoi & Company, Importers of Japanese Goods" (also visible on the NYPL archival photo),[105] a company mentioned in the January 17, 1923 *The Jewelers' Circular* 85, no. 2.[106] Underneath on the far right, it reads "Far East Trading Company Inc. N.Y."

Jewish Shoe Factory

On this cryptic ad in Williamsburg, the writing on this wall is in Yiddish, which uses Hebrew characters and a German syntax. Evidently, the last line says "produkten." Any other interpretations would be greatly welcomed. According to Moshe Rappoport from Zurich in a recent e-mail to me, "Apparently (I can't make out the first letter very clearly) it says 'Scouring Powder Products.' That would be like Ajax or Comet white powder cleanser products for washing dishes and pots. Since it was

used with food it would have had to have been Kosher. Do they still sell those tubular cans?"

Oh yes, Moshe, they do sell those tubular cans. However, the tubular gas silos seen in the distance near East Elmhurst are no longer on the landscape of the Long Island Expressway, but this sign still remains visible from the Hewes Street subway stop on the elevated J train platform on Broadway nearing the Brooklyn waterfront. A few of my friends who are scholars of Judaic studies and are fluent

in both Hebrew and Yiddish have been trying to decipher this ad. Of course, not all the letters are clear and in Yiddish, the vowels are omitted and every letter becomes more significant in denoting the meaning. The one letter that always drew my attention, as it was the most clearly visible, is the Hebrew letter aleph א, which is thought to be derived from the West Semitic word for "ox," and the shape of the letter derives from a Proto-Sinaitic glyph based on a hieroglyph depicting an ox's head, 𐤀.[107]

As a very young child, I would get dangerously high fevers and would become delirious. My mother would have to give me Phenobarbital to prevent seizures. I knew when I was getting the fevers when I would have the same recurring dream where this letter would appear to me on top of a large wooden gate to a horse corral that was closed and I could not open. This letter would sit defiantly on top of that gate. Since I did not grow up Jewish, I'm not quite sure how this letter appeared in my subconscious so early, although growing up in New York, I was exposed to Jewish culture by neighbors and friends. I also went to Jewish summer camps in the Catskills, where our counselors would tell us "Cropsey maniac" stories[108] to scare us around the campfire at night. I also remember hearing stories about a golem.

In Jewish folklore, the golem is an anthropomorphic being made from inanimate stuff that could be created to protect you in a time of great need. The creature came to life when the aleph was first carved into the golem's head to spell the word truth, or *emet*. To deactivate or kill the golem, you must remove the aleph, which then spells the word death, or *met*.[109] In a May 2009 *New York Times* article, it was said that "the Golem, according to Czech legend, was fashioned from clay and brought to life by a rabbi to protect Prague's 16th-century ghetto from persecution, and is said to be called forth in times of crisis."[110]

New York Magazine used this image to feature my show at the Williamsburg Art & Historical Society in December 2000, which was part of the worldwide Day without Art event on December 1 that was sponsored by the group Visual AIDS. During the preparation for this show, I was very debilitated from chemotherapy and radiation treatment for rectal cancer. In the show, I used very large reproductions (four feet by six feet), and hanging them was a very strenuous activity. Of course, I could not have done it without Vincenzo's help. I grappled with the concepts of truth (with a small "t") and death. Although the timing of this show seemed like it would have made it impossible for me to mount it, the exhibition became my golem. I didn't focus on my physical weakness from the treatment, nor did I focus on the pain from my surgery and the radiation. Instead, I remained focused on getting this show on the road. To this day, I keep an aleph under my bed just in case.

SUZY PERETTE'S DRESSES

Gigi Young originals.

Incorporated on April 6, 1938, as Lombardy Dresses, the company became known as Perette Dresses on January 18, 1950, and as Suzy Perette from January 31, 1958, to April 14, 1960.

"The Perette Silhouette" is a headless and limbless torso in a dress that hangs silently over the Garment District's West 37th Street like a two-dimensional coquette effigy. Meant to represent a dress on a dressmaker's mannequin, this towering image seems a bit uncanny. One of my favorite overheard comments at the NYHS was a conversation a woman had with her husband about Suzy Perette Dresses. When she walked in front of this image, she gasped and said, "I wore Suzy Perette Dresses. Anybody who was anybody wore Suzy Perette Dresses." She continued to describe some of the dresses she wore and the occasions for which she wore them. This elderly woman was transported back to a time when she was a young ingénue going out to a party with her friends. Many of these dresses were one of a kind and were only worn once.

WEBER & HEILBRONER

Stein Bloch clothes in the New York manner.

Weber & Heilbroner was a men's haberdashery from March 19, 1913, to June 27, 1979.

I overheard several people commenting about this establishment while this image hung at the New-York Historical Society show. Weber & Heilbroner was a rather posh haberdashery. One of the visitors actually worked there as a bookkeeper in the 1950s. In an interview with Manhattan borough historian Cal Jones, he fondly remembers shopping at the Weber & Heilbroner at Maiden Lane for a black woolen sweater with white trim. Cal described how the collar could be tucked in to make it look like a crewneck. According to Grutchfield:

OPPOSITE
Suzy Perette's Dresses—West 37th Street, Garment District, New York City. Taken March 1997. Ad circa 1950s. Hung in NYHS Exhibition.

BELOW
Weber & Heilbroner—West 35th Street, Herald Square, Garment District, New York City. Taken April 1997. Ad circa late 1950s. Hung in NYHS Exhibition.

Weber & Heilbroner, Haberdashers, were founded in 1902 by Milton Weber (1876–1936) and Louis Heilbroner (1878–1924). Louis Heilbroner, men's furnishing, was located at 920 3rd Ave. (corner of 53rd St.) in 1899. The original (1902) Weber & Heilbroner stores were located at 920 3rd Ave. and 757 Broadway (corner of 8th St.). Within a few years the business expanded to stores downtown at 58 Nassau St. (corner of Maiden Lane), 150 Nassau St., and 369 Broadway. A display ad[111] from the New York Times, 29 July 1904, mentions 58 Nassau St. & 757 Broadway. Also this one from the New York Times, 17 Sep. 1904. Weber & Heilbroner opened a store at 6th Ave./Broadway at 34th St. around 1923. Space in the Marbridge Building became available in 1922 when Rogers, Peet & Co., who had occupied the building from its inception, moved across 6th Ave. to the former Herald Building (New York Times, 18 April 1922). Weber & Heilbroner's store at 34th St. and 6th Ave./Broadway was one of four or five that survived until the 1970s when Weber & Heilbroner went out of business.[112]

Many of the incorporation dates I've included were found through the NYS Corporation's website (in the late '90s, there was an automated phone bank) and include when businesses were incorporated and why they went bankrupt. Many of these companies went bankrupt when they failed to pay their state corporate taxes. Weber & Heilbroner fell to this malady. The sign is still behind a large, stretchy mylar ad opposite Macy's at Herald Square. It is a bit hard to image just how large this sign is, until you look at the tiny yellow taxicabs and white moving trucks on the street below. I counted how many stories up I needed to be in order to shoot this sign from above. I counted lucky thirteen.

Upon ringing the service bell in the building lobby across the street on the north side of West 35th Street, I scanned the directory of the building while waiting for the doorman and noticed a business on the thirteenth floor called "Magnus" and told him I had an appointment with the manager. Naturally, the doorman called up and asked who I spoke with, and I said, "The girl at the front desk." The manager, Sheila, told him to let me up. When the elevator door opened up, Sheila was standing there with a young African American gay man who, before I could say hello, said, "Hi. I am the front desk girl, and WHO are YOU?" We all busted out laughing, and Sheila invited me in as I began to tell her about my desire to hang out one of her windows to get this shot. Although I was expecting resistance, she turned and said, "Thank goodness someone is documenting this. I love this sign. My office is right opposite it and I look at it every day. I think it's beautiful." She told me this as she started clearing coffee cups and inventory manifests from the windowsill. The window hadn't been opened in years, but she insisted on getting it open so I could get an unobscured shot. Sheila ordered pizza and soda. As we waited for lunch to arrive, I hung out of Sheila's window and snapped away. It was a "magnusly" memorable lunch engagement.

MISS WEBER MILLINERY

No. 48, Take Elevator.

Miss Weber had a millinery shop with an electric elevator. Miss Weber designed and manufactured hats in suite number forty-eight, and you didn't have to walk the stairs to get to her. *Inventors* writer Mary Bellis affirms that the electric elevator came into use toward the end of the nineteenth century, with the first one built in 1880 by the German inventor Werner von Siemens.[113]

According to Grutchfield, Ida L. Weber (1879–1932) was born in New York City, the daughter of Swiss immigrants Jacob and Regula Weber, and kept this hat-making shop here from 1911 through 1913 and then moved to 66 West 39th Street in New York's Millinery District. Miss Weber continued making hats there until about 1923, when she went out of business.[114] According to the University of Wisconsin Digital Collection, millinery and dressmaking were popular professions for women around the turn of the century, with the 1900 census reporting

Miss Weber Millinery—West 22nd Street, Flatiron District, New York City. Taken March 1997. Ad circa 1910. Hung in NYHS Exhibition.

338,144 female dressmakers, 138,724 seamstresses and 82,936 female milliners in the United States. This report stated that dressmaking ranked third, seamstressing ninth and millinery fourteenth "among occupations for women breadwinners."[115]

Oddly enough, the term "mad as a hatter" comes from eighteenth-century England, where millinery workers who used felt (which used mercury in processing the material) to make hats were subjected to long-term mercury exposure, resulting in dementia.[116] Countless women in New York City were subjected to perilous safety conditions making hats, shirts, dresses and other garments in factories that were run and owned by men. Miss Ida L. Weber ran her own company in a time when industry was totally dominated by male ownership, and I tip my hat to her. I worked as a dental office manager around the block from Miss Weber when I found this sign in the spring of 1997 tucked quietly in the entryway of 48 West 22nd Street, where she still greets passersby with a quiet downward glance.

R.H. MACY'S UPTOWN STABLES

Orders for goods taken here.

Try to imagine being a resident of Harlem at the turn of the century. Up until the 1880s, Harlem was like living in the suburbs, way north of all of the hustle and bustle of "the city." So I can only imagine that shopping for goods may have been a challenge, being so far away from the center of commerce. The elevated train lines were just being extended during a boom of development, but most of the major goods arrived on horse-drawn carriages from Midtown. To have a Macy's Uptown depot where you could place an order for a set of china and silverware must have been some luxury. The concept of a department store at the time was revolutionary. You didn't have to go to several stores to get what you needed; it was all under one roof. It was an invention of a late nineteenth-century entrepreneur who, like most Americans, didn't get it right the first time. Rowland Hussey Macy made a fifth attempt at opening a retail store in Manhattan in 1858 on Sixth Avenue near Fourteenth Street, which was "far north of the traditional retail market." Macy's Fourteenth Street location sold a whopping $85,000 worth of merchandise within one year. However, Macy's previous four attempts at establishing similar stores had "failed resoundingly," including the bankruptcy of his Haverhill store in Massachusetts.[117]

Apparently, Macy's success wasn't won alone, for at age thirty-six, the Quaker from Nantucket, Massachusetts, invited the Bavarian Jewish immigrant Lazarus Straus to run a kitchenware concession in the basement of his rapidly growing store, which was already "selling toys, candy, jewelry, hardware and men's furnishings." Straus, having

R.H. Macy's Uptown Stables—West 148th Street, Harlem. Taken March 1997. Ad circa 1900s. Hung in NYHS Exhibition.

already demonstrated "a sound reputation as a merchant in Georgia before moving with his family to New York in the aftermath of the Civil War,"[118] began selling china, porcelain, glassware and crockery in the Macy's cellar in 1873 at the behest of Lazarus's son Nathan. In 1884, the Straus family became part owners of the Macy's business. By 1896, the Lazarus family was sole owner of R.H. Macy's & Company. Lazarus's son Isidor "continued to run Macy's until his death, along with that of his wife Ida, on the 'Titanic' in 1912."[119]

After their demise on the *Titanic*, Isidor's sons took over the business and began the nationwide expansion of Macy's department stores after World War I.[120] Nathan Straus went on to establish Abraham & Straus in 1893, which ultimately acquired Macy's & Co. a century later. Today, at a Walmart, for example, you can buy all the food that you need for the week, some underwear for the kids, a sit-on power lawnmower and some shrubs to plant in your garden, get a pedicure and have your eyes examined for a new pair of glasses all in one giant consumer cavern, all on one floor! No stairs! And we owe our right to the one-stop shopping experience to the brainchild of R.H. Macy and, perhaps even more, to the business acumen of the Straus family.

HARRY'S DEPARTMENT STORE/AUFRECHT INSURANCE & REAL ESTATE

It's Harry's Department Store for the Greatest Values—Graham & Metropolitan Avenues

I've spent more time staring at this image in particular than almost any other sign I've documented. It is not for any other reason than that the four- by six-foot reproduction that hung at the WAH Center Exhibition in 2000 hangs in my office in my country home. I've often wondered who the man on the left was and where the large woman with the teal-colored sweat suit was going. At first, I didn't even realize there was a man on the left since the slide positive was scanned initially in the cardboard frame in which it is housed, which cuts almost a millimeter of information from the image, thus cropping it slightly. When the positive was removed from the cardboard sleeve to be scanned for this large-scale reproduction, suddenly the man in the short-sleeved polo shirt and gray slacks appeared.

Department store owner Harry also has been a mystery to me. There doesn't seem to be any mention of Harry's Department Store in any of the online archives I've searched. Kevin Walsh conveniently provided a link to the wedding announcement of Jacob M. Aufrecht[121] that was scanned and uploaded by Tom Tryniski in an extensive online archive he calls Old Fulton NY Post Cards.[122] Normally, this wedding announcement, which states the usual familial and temporal information, would seem quite unremarkable:

Berger—Aufrecht
   Miss Elise Berger, daughter of Mr. & Mrs. Emanuel Berger of 660 West 180th st., Manhattan, and Jacob M. Aufrecht, son of Mr. and Mrs. Marcus Aufrecht of 551 East 53d st., Brooklyn, will be married at the Hotel Astor on Sunday evening Oct 27, by Rabbi Alexander Lyons of the Eighth Avenue Temple.
   The bride will be attended by Miss Helen Welkersheimer. Max Abrams of Brooklyn will be the best man. Following a motor trip to Canada, the couple will reside at 551 East 53d st., Flatbush.

   Miss Berger is a graduate of Columbia University. Mr. Aufrecht is engaged in the real estate business.
   —*Brooklyn Daily Eagle, Sunday October 10, 1929*[123]

Totally mundane in its details, this wedding announcement would never have struck a chord unless I noticed the date that the bride and groom were to be wed. The Thursday afternoon before their wedding is known as Black Thursday (Black Friday in Europe due to the time difference). The Monday and Tuesday after their wedding are remembered as "Black" days as well. One could only wonder if the newlyweds ever went on their Canadian road trip after a nuptial weekend that landed smack in the middle of the stock market crash of 1929, precipitating the Great Depression. As I write this on a similar weekend, Standard & Poors downgraded the United States from a Triple A to an AA+ credit rating. Life goes on. Doesn't it?

Harry's Department Store/Aufrecht Insurance & Real Estate—Metropolitan and Grand Street Station, Williamsburg, Brooklyn. Taken August 1997. Ad circa 1940s.

Might as Well jUmP!

Reflections on the Color Blue

In early July 1998, I was seated in my office at a well-known direct marketer on Long Island when someone—I forget who—left a *New York Times* article on my desk. I was enraptured as I read about a man who was just as fascinated by the fading remnants of a forgotten New York as I was and documented his discoveries on the worldwide web, as it was known in those days. His name was Frank Jump, and he ran, and still runs, a website dedicated to the "faded ads" that dot New York City's landscapes.

The year 1998 was still the wild west days for what we now know as the Internet, but the web was beginning to assert itself as the Number One disseminator of information; where previously, amateur chroniclers had to finance and print up periodicals known as "zines" to get across their obsessions and desires, here was a golden opportunity for a cheap means of getting across what you wanted to say. The word "blog" hadn't been invented yet, but thousands of mavens were beginning to poke their heads above the muck and make their thoughts known worldwide. Today, bloggers influence elections, elect players to all-star games and influence the entertainment industry and everything else in every corner of life you can name, but in the late 1990s, it was mainly a hobbyists' forum.

So it was this incredible Frank Jump photograph of Reckitt's Blue that prompted me to sketch out on scrap paper what I wanted for *Forgotten New York* that memorable day in that direct marketing office. The circa 1890 ad for a laundry product manufactured by Reckitt's known simply as "Blue" was hidden for many years behind a building on Washington Avenue and Dean Street in Brooklyn; when the building was torn down, lo and behold: there it was. Reckitt's Blue happens to be my favorite shade of blue, by the way—and according to a *Forgotten* fan who wrote in to inform me, the color of the ad is: C-67.45 percent, M-34.9 percent, Y-7.84 percent, K-1.57 percent, taken from percentages from RGB monitor samples. The original color, considering the fade, may have been closer to C-74.51 percent, M-48.63 percent, Y-23.92 percent, K-10.59 percent.

I conceived of *Forgotten New York* out of the floating images of rusted lampposts, hidden alleys, bricked streets, ancient business signs, New York City neighborhoods that the guidebooks don't acknowledge such

Frank H. Jump and Kevin Walsh on May 1, 2005, at the Fading Ad Gallery.

as Georgetown, Eastchester, Throgs Neck, Winfield and Eltingville, as well as the ghost ads advertising long-deceased businesses that can still be found on walls all over the city. After seeing Frank's article and sketching out what components would make up *Forgotten New York*, I grabbed a camera (one I hadn't used for years) and set out snapping everything I remembered in my head that fit the *Forgotten New York* format. If you know what my early web pages looked like from those years ago, you also know

that I was a pretty crappy photographer in those days. I have since become a better one; I merely shoot on the sunny side now.

Of course, I soon contacted Frank, and he has become a staunch *Forgotten New York* ally over the years. The day I met him for the first time, what became Forgotten Tour #1 on June 1, 1999, he related the story of how he walked the el tracks on the J line in Bedford-Stuyvesant to better get a picture. I posted an image of ancient ad aficionado and daredevil

Frank Jump as he stands on top of a scaffold he had ascended in order to get better views of the Bushwick RKO.[124] Frank's pictures of the theatre also appear on his own website.[125] I have met many other people who have performed such daring feats to acquire just the right shot. Later that fall in Coney Island, at a lot on Surf Avenue and West 37th Street, a couple of ancient autos were for sale. (They needed a lot of rehabilitation.) Forgottoners gathered at a 1940s Olds, where Frank tried to give the old clunker a "jump" start.[126]

In May 2005, author and friend Dawn Eden published an article for the *Daily News* about fading ads, on which Jump and I collaborated.[127] Frank continues to limn ancient ads on his newer site, the *Fading Ad Blog*. Frank, a New York City teacher, has beaten cancer, is beating the HIV virus and married his lifelong partner, Vincenzo Aiosa, in 2004. He is also the uncle of Rosario Dawson[128]—we'll have to have Dawson on a Forgotten Tour sometime!

Kevin Walsh
Forgotten New York
July 10, 2008[129]

Laundry Products, Washing Machines and Real Estate

RECKITT'S BLUE

The Purest and Best.

Ultramarine. A perfect expression for what I felt the magical moment I first glimpsed this magnificent relic of the late nineteenth century—an azure monument to a pioneering advertising and global marketing campaign. Reckitt's Blue, a laundry whitener, was one of the first widely marketed laundry products manufactured by Reckitt & Sons, which was established in 1840 in Hull, England, by a Quaker named Isaac Reckitt. This laundry starch company began producing laundry blue in 1852 by using a combination of a synthetic ultramarine and sodium bicarbonate. Previously, the semiprecious stone lapis lazuli was ground to produce the active ingredient, so the advent of this synthetic made the product affordable to the masses. The naturally occurring blue pigment found in lapis was first discovered to be sodium aluminosulfosilicate in 1824 by the French chemist Jean-Baptiste Guimet. Guimet realized he could synthesize ultramarine by combining china clay, soda ash and trace sulfur.

Originally, the synthetic was imported from France or Germany, but after Isaac's death in 1862, Reckitt's sons began manufacturing it in Hull. After its introduction to the nascent global market, Reckitt's Blue soon outsold their original laundry starch and stove-blacking products. Stove blacking was produced from lead and used as a hearth polish. Reckitt & Sons also produced other liquid metal polishes (Brasso) and boot polishes. Reckitt's Blue is no longer manufactured in the United States.

My sister Jackie happened to be with me when I discovered this sign and suggested that I take the shot from the side. I kissed her goodbye and got in my car

PREVIOUS PAGES
Reckitt's Blue—622 Washington Avenue, Brooklyn. Taken March 1997. Ad was re-obscured as of April 2004. Ad circa 1890s. Hung in NYHS Exhibition.

OPPOSITE
Courtesy of Reckitt & Colman, Inc.

SPACE LATTICE DIAGRAM

OF

ULTRAMARINE BLUE

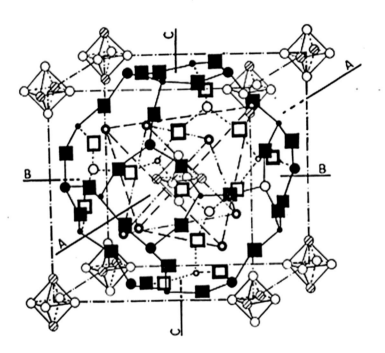

■ □ OXYGEN   ●○ ALUMINIUM

• ○ SILICON   ○ SODIUM

⊘ SULPHUR

slowly in an act of surrender. Suddenly, I shot out of the top of my head and was hovering in the cables of the Manhattan Bridge with a 360-degree view of Brooklyn and Manhattan. No longer in my body, I was free. Staring down at the car, I was immediately sucked back inside looking at the Manhattan skyline with the sun glinting off the windows of the World Trade Twins. Never have I felt such euphoria before without chemical assistance. It was a fleeting moment of bliss that seemed to last an eternity and a nanosecond all at once. I knew then and there that something very important was happening in my life. No longer would I obsess about my own mortality. Even four years later, when I was diagnosed with rectal cancer, I knew I would survive it if I just surrendered my anxiety.

Sadly, Reckitt's Blue has been re-obscured, sandwiched between the late nineteenth-century wall upon which it still remains and an eyesore some call urban renewal. This image has become iconic for me since it was the one the *New York Times* used for its feature on the campaign exhibit.

to have my film developed in Manhattan. When I got to the Manhattan Bridge, I got caught in a major mid-morning traffic jam. Anxious to get the film to the developers before noon for a two-hour turnaround, I started to get stressed out. I did not want the anxiety attack that I felt coming on, so I took a deep breath in and exhaled

P. ZACCARO REAL ESTATE/BENDIX HOME LAUNDRY PENTIMENTO

In a stunning piece of prose he wrote for the *New York Times* called "Olde York," David W. Dunlap describes the multilayered nature of New York as the following: "The city is not so much a tidy pile of building blocks as it is a chambered nautilus with walls of palimpsest on which the etchings of the present never entirely obscure the patterns beneath. Forever visible behind the newest layer, no matter how faint, are remnants of the civic past. New York does not forget."[130]

Usually, it is a challenge to decipher the two or more ads in a palimpsest—a word usually used to describe when a previously written text starts to ghostly appear from under another text written on top—but this P. Zaccaro/ Bendix one was very clear and remains clear to this day. This four-story mural dominates the Delancey Street access to the Williamsburgh Bridge while traveling east on Kenmare Street near the corner of Elizabeth. Although it roughly faces south, it has been protected by the sun's

destructive power by the shade of the building across the street.

The Bendix Home Appliance Corp was founded in 1936 by Judson S. Sayre and became the largest U.S. washing machine manufacturer by 1950.[131] Bendix introduced the first automatic front-loading washing machine in 1937 and secured the patent in 1939 with inventors John W. Chamberlin and Rex Earl Bassett Jr.[132]

P. Zaccaro's son, John Zaccaro—the husband of the late Geraldine Ferraro, former 1984 Democratic vice presidential nominee and U.S. House of Representatives member from New York— currently owns this real estate firm. Halfway down you can read the Bendix ad for washing machines that were probably sold at J. Eis and Sons. The telephone exchange Orchard-4 is a seven-digit number that was adopted in the 1940s, which is about when I would date this sign.

Here is an excerpt of a piece I wrote called "False Memories or Twisting at Two":

As a child I remember being fascinated by the washing machine in our kitchen. The rhythmic sound of the agitator going back and forth, back and forth, back and forth would mesmerize me. I would chant, "Wash-a-sheena, wash-a-sheena, wash-a-sheena…" while doing "the twist" all around the apartment. My mother Willy said I would throw all kinds of things in that old Bendix: pillows, forks, toasters, 45s, plants, cats—always transfixed by the washing machine blades going back and forth, back and forth…The spinning clothes became a cylindrical wall of

blur that was like its own form of matter like a plasma phase or excited energy state—an Einstein-Bose condensate. The centrifuge could not separate what was real from what was imagined. The forces of attraction were too strong.

Once, I got away from my mother at a State Fair in NY. My mother searched for me frantically. Finally she turned towards the stage at the prompting of a cheering crowd and there I was doing the twist to Chubby Checker's "Let's Twist Again." I also remember doing the twist on top of a bar in Amsterdam for American soldiers always chanting to myself—Wash-a-sheena, wash-a-sheena, wash-a-sheena…I have other false memories.

Today, Photoshop has become my centrifuge for separating fused memories. Usually when I'm trying to decipher a pentimento, I will select the section of the text and alter the hue and saturation, which sometimes helps to reveal the underlying ad. If you look carefully, just underneath the words "Real Estate, Brokerage, Management," the cubic image of a Bendix front-loading machine is clearly visible.

BENDIX HOME LAUNDRY

This is one of the many Bendix Home Laundry fading ads I've captured. A young family from Guyana was kind enough to let me climb out of their window onto an adjacent roof for this shot. Ironically, and with much delight, the Fading Ad Gallery was located directly across the street from this billboard and painted sign at 880 Bedford and 679 Myrtle for the almost two years that it was open. This also is one of the many MACK signs throughout the city. In February 2005, *Swindle Magazine*—a now defunct bi-monthly arts and culture publication founded in 2004 by artist Shepard Fairey—did a story on the gallery and this campaign. The photographer, Chris Glancy, thought it would be fun to get me to climb the billboard's catwalk and sit on the edge. This image can be seen on the campaign website.[133]

OPPOSITE
Bendix Home Laundry—Bedford and Myrtle Avenues, Brooklyn. Taken September 1998. Ad circa 1950s.

EMIL TALAMINI REAL ESTATE

ALgonquin 4-1817

In the 1954 film *It Should Happen to You,* starring Judy Holliday as Gladys Glover, an unemployed model uses the $1,000 she has saved up to rent a billboard in Columbus Circle, where she writes her name, motivated solely by the desire "to make a name for herself." The billboard is usually rented by the Adams Soap Company, which was late in reserving it. Through several twists and turns, she agrees to give the space over to the soap company in exchange for ten other billboard spaces around town, upon which she has her name written. New York City passersby start noticing Gladys's name and wonder, "Who is Gladys Glover?"

Who was Emil Talamini? It has been a great mystery to me since before I took this photograph. As a teenager, I would frequent Greenwich Village often. The view uptown on Sixth Avenue from Christopher Street was a familiar landscape that usually implied a night of fun in the city or perhaps a day

of protest, since the first gay and lesbian rights marches went up Sixth Avenue from Christopher Street. So when I took this photograph with the moon shooting out of the black stovepipe vent like from the barrel of a cannon, the mystery of *who was Emil Talamini* persisted to intrigue me. Finally, I have a clue. On October 29, 1970, the *New York Times* obituaries wrote about the death of Mr. Talamini:

Emil Talamini, of 70 East 10th Street, a real estate broker and investor long active in the Greenwich Village area, died yesterday in Memorial Hospital after a long illness. He was 64 years old.

Mr. Talamini was a 1928 graduate of Brown University. He was with Charles F. Noyes, Inc., and the William A. White & Sons before establishing his own real estate business. He was a member of the Real Estate Board, the New York Yacht Club and the Dunes Club of Narragansett, R.I.

He leaves his wife, the former Jeanette Jackson, and a stepson, Ronald Wills. [134]

Little else is available about Mr. Talamini besides his obituary and this sign for his business and telephone number showing the old New York City exchange—ALgonquin 4-1817. Mr. Talamini may be gone, but his name and old telephone number live on. No one who answers that telephone number knows anything about Mr. Talamini, and I'm sure they would love for the sign to be covered up by another billboard ad or perhaps even the name Gladys Glover, unless I'm the only curious and compulsive crackpot who calls this number asking about him.

OPPOSITE
Emil Talamini Real Estate—Sixth Avenue, Greenwich Village, New York City. Taken August 1997. Ad circa 1940s.

Jewelry and
Accessories

SHIELDS FINE JEWELRY

I could have been
One of these things first

I could have been a sailor
Could have been a cook
A real live lover
Could have been a book
I could have been a signpost
Could have been a clock
As simple as a kettle
Steady as a rock
—Nick Drake, "One of These
Things First"
Bryter Layter LP, 1970

Thanks to Grutchfield's tireless and remarkable research of the seemingly countless signs between 14th Street and 42nd Street, this ad's significance and the history of Shields Fifth Avenue's as a men's jewelry outlet was revealed. From the late 1940s until 1958, Shields was located at 302 Fifth Avenue near 31st Street. Shields then moved uptown to 401 Fifth Avenue at 37th Street. Shields closed its doors in New York City in the late 1960s; however, the name Shields Fifth Avenue lived on as a registered trademark of Watchbands Inc. of North Attleboro, Massachusetts. Wall dog Harry Middleton of Mack Sign Company painted this sign in the late 1940s. Grutchfield wrote that Bob Middleton said he had worked on this sign circa 1955, and according to Middleton, "with no windows, it was a rough job to paint."[135] Under this sign and somewhat obscured by the water tower, it also reads "Victor Porting Company."

In Tama Starr's *Signs and Wonders*, the first sentence on the first page she simply states, "Our signs tell us who we are." This is a level of signification that I've been tuned into for over fifteen years now. To some, other objects in our environment may also communicate an identity, or perhaps we may see ourselves personified in a building, a park or even a signpost. Looking south down Fifth Avenue with the Flatiron Building in the distance, you can still see the Bob Pins ad (see next ad) on the billboard facing north on the lower left. In 1979, Katherine Hepburn was asked in an interview with Morley Safer if she could be any building, which one would she be? She replied, "Most definitely, the Flatiron."[136] Also documented later in the Andrew Britton biography of *Katharine Hepburn: Star as Feminist*, Hepburn stated further: "Me, I'm like the

PREVIOUS PAGES
Shields Fine Jewelry—Fifth Avenue and West 33rd Street, Midtown, New York City. Taken April 1997. Original ad circa 1940s.

Flatiron Building. All I can say is I could never be anyone else. I don't want to be anyone else, and I've never regretted what I've done in my life, even though I've had my nose broken a few times doing it."[137]

In 1987, when I was living with my former partner, activist and real estate developer Eric Sawyer, he told me about the time he ran into Ms. Hepburn in Morningside Park after the city had completed a major landscape renovation project there. Sawyer thought he had seen Hepburn turning a corner to go down the stairs into the park, and then heard a cane being dropped and banging down the stairs. Sawyer rushed around the corner to look and see if Hepburn was OK, and there she was, picking up the cane and exclaiming in her faltering graciousness, "Oh, this was once such a glorious park. We used to come here, Spencer and I, and eat a boxed lunch on a blanket over there." She pointed to a tree in the distance and continued, "This park had fallen into such disrepair for so long, I had to come see what they have done to restore it."

Hepburn asked Sawyer what he was doing in the neighborhood, and he told her he had recently bought a Harlem brownstone in an auction and was restoring it. Hepburn asked if he minded telling her how much he had paid for it. Without flinching, Sawyer told her, and she shared how much she had paid for her Turtle Bay residence back in the 1930s. Hepburn then asked if she could see the brownstone, and Sawyer, rather amazed, said, "Sure! Now?" Hepburn signaled for her driver, and a late 1970s blue Chevy Impala pulled up, and off they went to his brownstone on Manhattan Avenue, which was under reconstruction.

One Saturday morning when I was living with Sawyer, the phone rang and woke me up. I answered groggily, and I heard that unmistakable voice on the other end: "Good morning, this is Kate Hepburn, is Eric Sawyer available?" I said, "Yes, Ms. Hepburn, I'll get him right away." She said, "Please, call me Kate." I jumped out of bed and got him.

Hepburn's identification with a New York City landmark building is quite astounding, since I, too, have identified myself with fading ads, which are landmarks in their own right. Having to choose one sign in particular would be a hard decision since so many of these signs mean so many different things to me. Here's my dilemma—there is my first sign, Omega Oil, and my first true love, Reckitt's Blue. Hepburn's ability to be so sure about the Flatiron speaks to her self-confidence and self-awareness—the recognition of the power she had as a person, as a woman and as a public figure. It also speaks to the power a building, or even a signpost, may have on an individual. These signs as part of our urban landscape have both external and internal significance and, as Starr states, "tell us who we are." Which makes it so much more evident how the disappearance of these landmarks can be devastating. Hepburn was and continues to be a human landmark, and I think of her every time I pass by or even think about the Flatiron Building. She will be sorely missed. In retrospect, since there isn't any one particular sign with which I could identify myself, I believe I need to err on the side of Christopher Isherwood's sentiment—"I am a camera."

BOB PINS FRESCO

Bob pins or bobby pins were first used in the 1920s to keep the new bob-style hairdo in place. The trademark for the bobby pin was held for several decades by the Bob Lépine Corp of Buffalo.[138] This cheerful fresco must have been from the early1940s, as it contains deco-esque style elements. High above Fifth Avenue in the shadows of the Empire State Building, this ad sits above a roof of a carpet retailer that was only accessible due to my political proclivities. Upon entering the business, I was greeted by the owner, a short, well-dressed elderly Jewish man. I started my spiel. "Are you aware of the vintage sign outside of your building?" Sign? What sign? So I explained what I perceived as a bobby pins ad from the '40s that I could only get access to if he let me onto his roof for just a minute. I was wearing one of my Dinkins campaign buttons, and he exclaimed, "You look like a nice boy and you're a Democrat." Ironically, the man's yarmulke was being held down by a bobby pin. Last I looked, these two happy Caucasian faces are still smiling faintly northward at the Empire State Building.

GRIFFON SHEARS AND MACK SIGN COMPANY SPOTLIGHT

This is one of the most photographed fading ads that the Mack ad company produced. Grutchfield wrote that the Griffon Cutlery Works was founded by Albert L. Silberstein in 1888. Griffon manufactured "razors, nail files and a great many types of scissors, including pinking shears, nippers and manicure sets, as well as 'Ladies' Button Hole' scissors." According to the Griffon trademark registration, embroidery scissors, poultry shears, barber shears, tweezers, pushers, blackhead removers and nose scissors were also manufactured goods. Harry Middleton painted this colossal and magnificent ad about 1939 or later. In the 1940s, Griffon became incorporated, and the sign was repainted to represent the change in the company name from "Works" to "Corp." During the 1960s, Griffon left New York City for Inwood, New York, on Long Island while maintaining a showroom at 385 Fifth Avenue.[139]

In a July 9, 1998 article, "Saving Images of 'Dead Sign' on Old Walls," written about me by Randy Kennedy for the *New York Times*, he opens his "Public Lives" piece with the following:

"Tweezers, nippers, manicure sets," says Frank H. Jump, reading slowly, his head craned back in a familiar stance. He is on West 19th Street near Seventh Avenue staring up at a fading, chiaroscuro advertisement painted on a building by a long-gone company called Griffin [sic] Shears. The ad outlasted the business, but like hundreds of the city's so-called dead signs—murals for extinct goods or companies, painted high on brick walls—it is fast disappearing.[140]

OPPOSITE, TOP
Bob Pins fresco—West 32nd Street, Midtown, New York City. Taken August 1997. Hung in NYHS Exhibition.

OPPOSITE, BOTTOM
Griffon Shears and Mack Spotlight—West 19th Street and Seventh Avenue, Chelsea, New York City. Taken September 1997. Ad circa 1950s.

Savings,
Loans and
Fur Vaults

THE GREATER NEW YORK SAVINGS BANK

This is a remnant of a time when smaller local savings banks flourished. The Greater New York Savings Bank was established in 1897. In 1964, it merged with the City Savings Bank of Brooklyn, which was then acquired by the Flatbush Savings Bank in 1970. Finally, in 1997, Flatbush Savings was acquired by Astoria Federal Savings Bank.[141] The fingers logo is reminiscent of the "let your fingers do the walking" Yellow Pages ad campaign, which didn't make the top ten best slogans of the century but did place as honorable mention for slogans of the century at *Advertising Age*'s website.[142] On September 25, 2004, the *New York Times* printed this obituary about the creator of this campaign:

> *Stephen Baker, who created the "Let your fingers do the walking" ad campaign for the Yellow Pages and advised readers on how to live with a neurotic dog, died in Manhattan on Sept. 13. He*

was 83. The cause was cancer of the gastrointestinal tract, his son Scott, said. As an art director for the advertising agency Cunningham & Walsh and later as founder of his own firms, Mr. Baker tried to create sassy ads that steered clear of the hard sell.

For one commercial in the "Let your fingers do the walking" campaign to promote AT&T's Yellow Pages, a woman's well-manicured hand saunters down a street, its long red fingernails resembling high heels. AT&T used the slogan for at least six years.

"Baker was part of what was then known as the creative revolution," said Fred Danzig, a former editor of Advertising Age. "He was one of the people who I suppose you might say was at the forefront of it."[143]

My original caption for this was "A picturesque cobblestone street in one of Brooklyn's more isolated neighborhoods known for its tough waterfront residents and fabulous views of Lady Liberty." Since then, this neighborhood has become a hotbed of shopping opportunities, with a Fairway market being built on the waterfront, as well as a giant IKEA. The Brooklyn Waterfront Artists Coalition also opened a waterfront gallery since this building with the Fingers Walking logo was torn down. Now in its place is a community garden, another urban green feature that is always at risk of becoming new real estate.

PREVIOUS PAGES
Ash's Certified Cold Storage—Bronx. Taken August 1997. Ad circa late 1950s.

OPPOSITE
The Greater New York Savings Bank—Red Hook, Brooklyn. Taken June 1998. Building now nonexistent. Ad circa early 1960s.

J.J. FRIEL LOANS

Joseph John Friel was born on March 15, 1853. He emigrated from County Donegal, Ireland, in 1875 and came to the United States with five dollars in his pocket. Soon, Friel got a job as a ditch digger in a construction company in Bedford-Stuyvesant, Brooklyn. When digging a ditch one day in the hot sun, he looked up at a beautiful house at 699 Willoughby Avenue and proclaimed that he would one day own it. His supervisor thought Friel must have been suffering from heat prostration and made him sit down and rest. After being a ditch digger, Friel worked faithfully for several years for a pawnbroker on Grand Street. Friel had made arrangements with his boss to buy the business from him "on time." By the time his boss died, Friel had begun to grow this brokerage company into a million-dollar business.

According to the Brooklyn Genealogy Website, J.J. Friel ran a pawnbroker business between the years 1880 and 1890 at 86 Myrtle Avenue off Duffield Place,[144] where the new Metrotech Building high-rise casts its shadow on the Flatbush Avenue extension.

J.J. Friel Loans—Coney Island Avenue near Caton Avenue. Taken March 1999. Ad circa 1950s.

An additional office was listed at 989 Myrtle Avenue between Sumner and Throop where there is now a New York City Housing Project. Both addresses no longer exist. A *New York Times* obituary states that Joseph John Friel started in the pawn brokerage business on Grand Street in 1870.[145] Numerous signs for this business can be found from Park Slope, Brooklyn, to Jamaica Queens. This sign on Coney Island Avenue in the Kensington section of Brooklyn, however, no longer sees the light of day.

Recently, a family member of Friel, Michael Hughes (great-grandson), of Detroit, Michigan, contacted me about the whereabouts of the Park Slope J.J. Friel sign I had posted on my blog. Hughes spoke about the possible restoration of the sign and got me in touch with his aunts, Friel's surviving grandchildren— DeDe Burke of Mount Kisco, New York, and Aileen Schaefer of Islip, New York. Almost all the historical and genealogical information on Friel was gleaned through these telephone interviews with Friel's descendants.

In 1898, Friel married Frances Noonan, and by 1903, at age fifty, he and his wife had a daughter, Mary Margaret Friel. J.J. Friel died in May 1914 at age sixty from pneumonia in his home at 699 Willoughby Avenue. Mary Margaret, who inherited the family fortune upon her father's death, went on to graduate from Manhattanville College in 1924 and to marry Henry Mannix in 1926. Henry Mannix became a partner in the law office of White & Case, which was already a legendary Wall Street firm. Mary Margaret and Henry Mannix had ten children, nine of whom lived to adulthood. According to Friel's granddaughter Aileen, the Friel business continued to be run by the family well into the 1970s. Friel was buried in Holy Cross Cemetery in Brooklyn.

After getting off the phone with a family member and realizing how closely Friel was buried to where I lived, I immediately cut some flowers from my garden and headed over to the cemetery on my Vespa. After a three-minute ride, I picked up a map from the cemetery office, where they had kindly written the names of the family members buried at the plot with the years of their birth and death, and placed the flowers on the Friel-Mannix family burial ground. It seems almost unfathomable that this man, whose name I've known for over fifteen years and about whom I knew next to nothing, was buried 1.2 miles from my home, and I now have contact with his family ninety-seven years after his death.

Solemnly, I stood in front of the Friel tombstone while "Taps" was played at a funeral procession nearby. I cannot begin to describe how deeply profound and moving this experience was for me. The tombstone bore the many names of members of the Friel-Mannix family, beginning with the Friels' first child, a son named James who died at birth in 1899. Mary Margaret Friel was thereby their second child and their only child. Having lost her father at the age of ten, she lived a rich and full life with forty-eight grandchildren to recount their great-grandfather's legacy. I returned home and spoke on the phone with the eldest living daughter of Mary Margaret, Aileen Schaefer. We spoke about faith, trust and surrender. We spoke about the remarkable circle of life that brought us to this telephone conversation and life's mysteries. I feel honored to take part in the telling of their story. Perhaps one day in the next century this sign will be exposed again and the story of J.J. Friel will come to light yet again.

LOANS

Diamonds, Jewelry, Clothing, Furs

Loans—Flushing Avenue, Brooklyn waterfront in Williamsburg. Taken August 1997.

Will building New York ever be finished? As long as there are loans, there will be renovation. What is remarkable about this image is it documents a time when the Brooklyn waterfront was still not very accessible to the public. Since this picture was taken, so many changes have occurred in this part of Brooklyn. Williamsburg has become a youth mecca, mostly students from NYU and other prestigious educational institutions, the neighborhood has exploded with bars, restaurants and galleries. The waterfront is seeing some of the more upscale new residential buildings, and the area has become one of the hottest neighborhoods in America, let alone New York City.

Still, many lower-income families have become displaced by this rapid and meteoric gentrification. The neighborhood suffered initially, like most Brooklyn waterfront neighborhoods such as Red Hook and Sunset Park, from the building of the Brooklyn-Queens Expressway and the Gowanus Expressway. The block behind this was where Gabila Knishes originated. I went back there today, and the entire block has been bulldozed. Gabila's moved to Copaigue, Long Island. Like most other industries on Brooklyn's waterfront, it has been moved to somewhere more affordable. Brooklyn's waterfront is finally allowing public access, with parks that stretch along the East River from Red Hook to Greenpoint. Luxury apartments are also dotting the riverfront, rivaling Manhattan's riverfront assortment of posh digs.

ASH'S CERTIFIED COLD STORAGE

"Safe as a Bank" Cypress 2—0200

The National Cold Storage building on Brooklyn's waterfront, one of the largest cold storage warehouses in New York, was recently torn down to build the Brooklyn Bridge Park at Old Fulton Street Landing. An image of this building can be seen on the *Fading Ad Blog*.[146] Not to be confused with refrigeration of edible perishables, cold storage was a service offered after World War II across North America for women's fur preservation. This April 11, 1944 ad from the *Ottawa Evening Citizen* best explains the need for "cold storage" with its persuasive ad copy:

Proper Storage Protects Your Fur Coat Investment
Furs lose the oils that keep skins supple, in warm air. They require careful cleaning to remove dust and possible moth larvae, then storage in low temperature with the right degree of humidity. Such care lengthens the life of your coat, protects your fur investment, as no other care will do.

When you buy a bond you immediately put it in a safety deposit box or some other place equally safe and accessible. What about your furs? They represent a VERY CONSIDERABLE sum of money, yet, perhaps, you leave them in your apartment during the warm summer months, without special cleaning and other care, and wonder why that lovely coat appears dull and lifeless and brittle-feeling when you come to don it again in the autumn.

Give us the opportunity to store your coat. Our fur storage vaults give perfect protection. Insurance covers every loss possibility and is world wide. The cost? Very low indeed. Only 2% of your own valuation.—M. Caplan Ltd. 195½ Sparks St.[147]

Brush Up
Business
WITH
Paint
Paste
Paper
AND
Brush

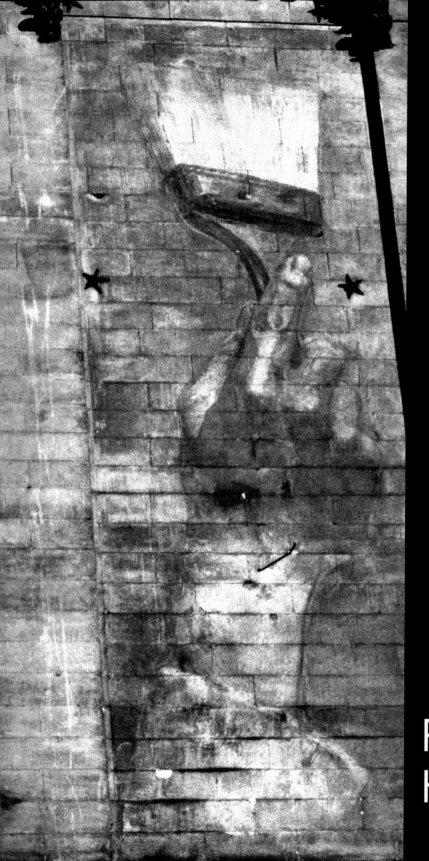

Paint and
Hardware

Eaglo Paint Seasonal Quadripartite

Signs and vines weather and grow.
Brick, pigment, plant and
lime—
Tenuously intertwined through
time.
As paint degrades and image fades,
Soft tones evolve
From salmon pinks and jades—
Into sand and grime.
—Frank H. Jump, July 2000

This sign on Nostrand Avenue and Glenwood Road, near Brooklyn College, illustrates the effects of nature on a fading ad, making it a dynamic reminder of the passing of time—not to mention one's own mortality. The last image was taken on June 22, 1999, and is an unusual summer state for this entwining symbiosis of signage and vinage. Apparently, the roots were cut, and the healthy, lush leaves have withered in the summer sun—another unexpected death.

George Carey Simos (University of Wales, Aberystwyth)[148] published on the web in 2000 a very comprehensive thesis on photography called "Are Photographs Copies of the World?" that includes the Eaglo Paint Quadripartite. Simos's introduction:

Are photographs copies of the world, or do they represent the photographer's interpretation of the world, as Susan Sontag mentions in her book, "On Photography"? The answer to this question does not only lie in our daily lessons about visual perception, but also in the written theories about how we read images or interpret them. I will be examining these later.

It is clear, that the world around us is extremely complex and visually mind-boggling. What is seen every day forms every individual's interpretation of his or her world. Every day across the globe, people decide to frame a part of this "interpretation" to make it last forever—or at least as long they are around to see it. The role of the photographer is the same, just like the painter who "captures" a moment in time, in reality or imagination, with his paintings. The photographer is also such an artist, who may capture "a moment," "a moment in time" as he or she perceived it—in this case how he or she "interpreted" it. When the camera lens clicks and burns the image onto photographic film, it is as if the photographer is "painting," or "drawing" his or her interpretation of the moment. This takes place because of the variables involved in taking a photograph. These may include the camera, the lighting, the angle, the shutter speed, the film, or the film speed. Choosing all the above, the photographer becomes the artist choosing his or her paints, paper, and brushes.

In this essay, I would like to delve deeper into the idea of photographs as "interpretations" of the world as Susan Sontag once famously wrote, and will attempt to describe the considerations that the artist/photographer makes in each instance. At this point I would like to introduce my examples, their uses, and their characteristics.

This series of seasonal photographs was taken by Frank Jump, a photographer in New York, who wanted to show his interpretation of the fading memories of the 1930's adverts in New York City. He chose to freeze these moments from the same angle every season, to illustrate how we interpret the same subject in different seasonal states. These photographs perhaps represent the artist's nostalgia for the past. Because of this we can assume that he was making a record of something, a selection from his interpretation of the environment around him. The moment he froze on four occasions is unique to itself as

is the way the photographer perceived it when he took the photographs.

—Making a Record—
Making a record is one of the most popular purposes for the photographic medium. The photographer decides that what he or she sees and perceives, and what is worth recording. The photographer follows this purpose (recording), photographing events, or processes. The final product is therefore a record of the photographer's interpretation of the event, or process. A good example of making a record, is the collection of photographs by both Frank Jump, and David Modell found on the picture-page of this study. Frank H. Jump photographs the building at different seasons, to record the changes that the seasons bring about. He is thus recording a process. David Modell on the other hand is recording social conditions in a particular time period in history. He is recording an event.[149]

When I first noticed and photographed the Eaglo Paint sign in Flatbush in June 1998, it was covered in a green carpet of leaves, with just the bottom

left peeking out. This sign became a friendly landmark on my walk home from the train station at Brooklyn College, and I was happy to see it every day, waiting patiently for me to notice it. By the fall, the leaves had turned a bright crimson, and I stood in the same spot where I had shot it in June to document its fiery display. In December, the vines were already defoliated, and the detail of the sign became even more apparent. I took another shot in the dead of winter from the same spot. By the spring of 1999, I thought about taking the shot. In the interim, someone, perhaps the owner of the building, had severed the roots from the stem of the vines, and the leaves turned quickly to a pallid sepia. So I took the shot again with the dying vine, not knowing what was planned for that wall. Within a few weeks, the vines were scraped from the wall and the sign was mortared over and then covered with a water-resistant silver paint, its process of fading into obscurity stopped.

Often, people have asked why so many of the older ads have lasted so long, and I usually tell them it's the lead paint that was used back

Eaglo Paint—Brooklyn. Ad circa 1950s.

Left to right: Taken summer 1998; fall 1998; winter 1998; spring 1999.

then. In examining the lists of chemicals that constituted what was in paints marketed for home use, the toxicity levels are staggering. I learned from a buddy of mine with a vast knowledge of chemicals and dyes,[150] Robert Baptista (*The Despair of Port Arthur, TX*),[151] whom I had met through the *Fading Ad Blog*, that the Eaglo Paint and Varnish Corp had a home right here in New York City. Baptista wrote the following information to me in an e-mail:

The Eaglo Paint and Varnish Corporation was located at 49-20 Fifth St. in Long Island City. It was established in the early 1900s. Herbert E. Hillman was Technical Director for many years.

Attached [below] is an ad for Eaglo Paint that appeared in the Bridgeport Post *on May 11, 1973.*

The New York–New Jersey metropolitan area was home for many of the largest paint manufacturers such as Sherwin-Williams and Benjamin Moore. The raw materials for paint, namely pigments, solvents, resins and additives, were readily available from local industries.[152]

As director of Eaglo Paints, Herbert E. Hillman was named in 1953 in a lawsuit involving lead poisoning, in which twenty cases of childhood lead poisoning resulted in five fatalities.[153] In another publication about house paints, Harriet A.L. Standeven wrote that Eaglo Paint and Varnish Corporation's Magic Satin product, which was introduced in October 1952, contained a highly carcinogenic substance called alkyd-modified styrene-butadiene, which, while making the paint slower to dry, increased its durability. Standeven concluded by saying, "Today the addition of an alkyd resin is considered deleterious, although the practice continued until the 1990s."[154]

BRUSH UP BUSINESS WITH PAINT, PASTE, PAPER & PUSH

(pages 150–151)

This beauty of a sign remains one of the best untouched ads in New York City. Just a few blocks north of Ground Zero, this TriBeCa treasure is perhaps a remnant of an early home improvement and office supplies campaign. Or is it? The style of this ad, with the block font and shading, is indicative of the 1910 style of ads. But most of the ads I've documented from this period, especially the ones facing south or west toward the blazing sun, have faded beyond recognition. As much as I wanted this to be an authentic ad, I've always been dubious. In a May 2009 blog posting, Jeremiah Moss of *Jeremiah's Vanishing New York* made the following observations:

This is a landmark building. The blog Haute Notes wrote extensively on its history, which dates back to 1860: "By the time of the First World War, photos show fine etched-glass entry doors and a sweeping canopy sheltering Vogric's Café. Its Slovenian owner advertised the Knickerbocker beers and ales brewed in Manhattan by Colonel Jacob Ruppert."

Most curious are the seeming ghost signs on the facade, which show a giant hand holding a paint brush and the words: "Brush Up Business with Paint, Paste, Paper, & Push." (Here, "push" means to sell, writes Forgotten NY.)

Frank Jump, in his excellent ghost sign blog, dates the signage to the 1910s. But Haute Notes writes, "the signs don't appear in any of the historic photos, even those from the 1940s."

Was the ghost sign somehow uncovered? Or was it put there later on, maybe for a 1970s movie, and made to look like the 1910s?

Whatever the story, it seems one of two things will happen to this building: Bouley will eventually move in or it will be demolished. Either way, we'll probably lose the signage, as we lost the Delphi, a once-strong survivor in a vanishing part of town.[155]

Now that the fading ad enthusiasts' network has grown, the detective work has become a shared task. I value the collaboration, as loose as it may be at times, with other documentarians. Of course, the Internet has revolutionized the way we disseminate images and information about these images.

W.W. Grainger

Unless you are a building contractor, or married to one like me, you probably have never heard about W.W. Grainger, an industrial supplies company established in 1924—that still is in business! It is also another company that hired the prolific Mack team to paint its sign.

W.W. Grainger—Canal Street, SoHo, New York City. Taken August 1998. Ad circa late 1960s.

Horse
and
Carriage

J.A. KEAL'S CARRIAGE MANUFACTORY & REPAIR

When this sign was exposed, I received a call from David W. Dunlap at the *New York Times* to get a shot of this before it was covered up again. Joseph Berger of the *Times* wrote this about the sign in an article called "Fading Memories" in 2005:

The tearing down of old buildings in Times Square has given some once-obscured old signs a fleeting exposure. One of the last signs in the area—for J.A. KEAL'S CARRIAGE MANUFACTORY REPAIRING on Broadway and 47th Street—was suddenly revealed around 1998 when the adjacent building was torn down. But it was concealed again the next year once a new building began rising on the same spot. [156]

Of all the ads I've photographed, J.A. Keal's Carriage Manufactory & Repair best illustrates the collision of two advertising eras and serves as a time capsule. This image also resonates with the motivation and urgency I have that drives this campaign. The banner on the lower left reads: "Broadway Cares/ Equity Fights AIDS," which is "one of the nation's leading industry-based, nonprofit AIDS fundraising and grant-making organizations." Since 1988, BC/EFA "has raised over $195 million for essential services for people with AIDS and other critical illnesses across the United States by drawing upon the talents, resources and generosity of the American theatre community." [157]

Above that on a building is an ad that was designed to mimic a ticker-tape news caption, which documents the shows that were being advertised in this theatre-driven neighborhood. The dazzling, optically illusive Levi's ad is just to the right of that. The image is split almost in half, with the left side a portal on the late twentieth century and the right side a window onto the late nineteenth century. Kevin Walsh makes these comments on his *Forgotten New York* website: "It stood there like a ghost, as if to mock the high tech/neon ads that currently decorate the Great White Way. The contrast between advertising techniques of the 1880s and 1990s is striking. Keal's ad was painted there in the era of gaslights, when the auto was yet to be invented and horses were still the prime means of transportation." [158]

CARRIAGES, COUPES AND HANSOMS

Built in 1870, 109 West 17th Street is another example of how New York was once a horse town. On Walter Grutchfield's site, for which I provided this image and an additional image adjacent to this window, he claims, "The building was, in fact, a livery stable kept by Patrick Logan from approximately 1900 to 1905." Grutchfield, who had been diligently documenting and researching vintage ads from 14th to 42nd a decade before me, said, "Until I saw these on Frank's web site, I had been unaware of their existence. But there they were, and on a building right next door to the old B&H! I must have walked past them a hundred times without seeing them."[159]

The elusiveness of fading ads is what makes this campaign so intriguing. In an August 2010 article by Nick Hirshon of the *New York Daily News*, Kathleen Hulser of New-York Historical Society said, "Ghost signs draw your attention to things that are often below the level of consciousness."[160] An older gentleman who lives in Manhattan and walks down this street every day made me aware of this sign. Eager to get the best shot of it, I had to wait until a double-parked Fed Ex truck moved out of the way. Then it dawned on me what I needed to do. This moment was documented in Randy Kennedy's "Public Lives" article about me in the *New York Times*:

On West 17th Street, he [Jump] climbed atop a Federal Express truck while the driver was away to get a shot of a tiny mural for a kind of rent-a-car garage of its day, on a red-brick building that now houses a store selling expensive Japanese screens. The sign says, "To Let, Carriages, Coupes, Hansoms," and "Victoria's Light Wagons, Horses Taken in Board by the Month."

"The driver came back and he said 'You get the hell off there.' And I said very nicely, 'I just need a minute or two more, thanks.'"[161]

Often, I have to just go for it, because asking permission doesn't always work. Once, I asked a business owner in Bed-Stuy Brooklyn if I could get on the roof of

her antique shop, which she told me she had owned for over thirty-five years, to shoot a vintage cigarette ad. The woman looked at me dubiously and asked, "What ad?" I took her by the hand and led her outside and pointed to the sign, to which she exclaimed, "Oh snap." Then she wanted to know what was so important about photographing these signs. I told her she had owned this shop for thirty-five years and never realized this sign was above her. That's why this is such an important subject to document. Unfortunately, the FedEx driver didn't want to hear it when he saw me on top of his truck. C'est la guerre.

PREVIOUS PAGES
J.A. Keals Carriage Manufactory & Repair—47th and Broadway, New York City. Taken April 1998. Ad circa 1877. Hung in NYHS Exhibition.

LEFT
Carriages, Coupes and Hansoms—109 West 17th Street, Chelsea, New York City. Taken August 1997. Ad circa early 1900s. Hung in NYHS Exhibition.

Fuel, Oil,
Gas and
Coal

DIANA COAL & OIL

Incorporated from December 7, 1955, through March 25, 1981.

If you've ever taken Atlantic Avenue going east toward South Conduit on your way to John F. Kennedy Airport or out to the Long Island beaches, you would have seen this silo on the south side as you were turning right onto Conduit. Written in a message thread in a forum on Trains dot com: "Their coal silos were a landmark on Atlantic Avenue for decades—a quick check of Bing shows the silos are no more, the address (3298 Atlantic Ave) being a big empty field roughly where Conduit intersects Atlantic."[162]

I used to teach in a middle school nearby and witnessed the demolition of Diana Coal & Oil. The documentation of the process was included in the school yearbook for I.S. 171 Abraham Lincoln Middle School in 2003. Diana Coal & Oil's demise was also documented on the *Fading Ad Blog*.[163] Six years earlier, I had flipped the bird to angry drivers as I stood in the middle of Atlantic Avenue to get this shot, car horns blaring from all sides. Speaking of birds, Diana Coal & Oil was the home of thousands of pigeons. The silos, aside from being a landmark, were a health risk, since they were easily accessible from the street and children would climb inside, where bird droppings literally coated every surface available. The eight cylindrical cement towers stood at least ten stories high and were seen long before you got to the intersection.

PARAGON OIL

Oil certainly has been in the news these days. Between the wars being fought over the control of oil, oil company mergers, the price of oil going up dramatically and down slightly and, worst of all, the horrific spills in the gulfs and bays around the world, you are bound to be slipping on some oil story somewhere. In doing research for this book, I've found that I'm partially responsible for personally polluting the ocean of information on the Internet, as whenever I do a search for a particular product or business, my photographs come up rather early in the results. I'm not complaining, since many a webmaster has paid good money to get his or her website placed in the top Google searches. So when I went to do my research on Paragon Oil, my photo made the top ten.

Interestingly enough, the Paragon Oil website hit number one. So when I went to its site to find out about the history of this family business, there was another immigrant story looking to live the American dream, right next to my photograph—without a photo credit! When I called the company to tell them I would be quoting their family story, the receptionist said, "Don't you need permission for that?" So I made a trade.

[Paragon] was founded in the early twentieth century in New York City by five brothers: Henry, Irving, Robert, Benjamin, and Arnold Schwartz. The brothers, and their sister Bess, were first-generation Americans; their parents were Jewish immigrants from the town of Belaya Tserkov, near Kiev, today located in the Ukraine. Their father Sam was a blacksmith, and relatives back in Ukraine were involved in the whale oil business.

PREVIOUS PAGES
Diana Coal & Oil—Atlantic Avenue, Brooklyn. Taken March 1997. Hung in NYHS Exhibition.

BELOW
Paragon Oil—Long Island City, Queens. Taken September 1997. Ad circa 1950s.

The combination of these factors led to the brothers experimenting with building the first oil heaters designed for residential buildings.

Paragon Oil was primarily a fuel oil distribution business, *operating a fleet of trucks around the Northeastern United States. It continued in operation until the 1950s, when it was modernized. Today Paragon Oil leads the industry with a fleet of 57* *fuel oil trucks delivering to homes and businesses.*[164]

My photo still adorns their history page and now says "photocredit" next to my image. Now *that's* progress.

OIL HEATS BEST (COSTS LESS)

Oil heat claims to be more ecologically friendly. The fuel is more efficient and can cost less than gas. According to an energy website, "Because oil requires more sophisticated burner systems than gas does to be fired efficiently, oil-fired heating appliances typically cost more than their gas-fired competitors."[165] This sign, a remnant of the gas v. oil heats best ad campaigns, is a great example of what I call an urban ediglyph—the interplay between a fading ad and graffiti. Usually, an ediglyph is when the graffiti and fading ad are part of the same wall, creating a synthesis of building wall (edi, as in ediface) and glyph (as in petroglyph) with the graphic of an ad and the graphic of a graffiti tag or street art.[166]

This block on White Plains Road in the Bronx served as a giant canvas for local graffiti artists. What is fascinating is how these voracious graffiti taggers left the Oil Heats Best sign alone. With few exceptions, these street artists tend to leave the work of the wall dogs uncovered and much prefer to cover the work of rival taggers. Where the two works of art collide—the ancient painted message of a long deceased commercial artist and the cryptic message or cartoon image of a spray paint artist—a uniquely significant ediglyph is created. The best example of this is a wall in DUMBO (Down Under the Manhattan Bridge Overpass) near the Fulton Ferry Landing on Adams Street. A large brick face with an old warehouse name painted on the side of the building was used as a canvas for a graffiti artist who painted what looked like schematic drawings of surveying instruments, gear-cranked machines and the barrel of a shotgun. These images are on the Exhibition Archives page that documents the shows we had at the Fading Ad Gallery.[167]

OPPOSITE
Oil Heats Best (Costs Less)— White Plains Road near 241ˢᵗ Street, Wakefield, the Bronx. Taken May 1997. Ad circa 1950s. Hung in NYHS Exhibition.

BUY TEXACO/SPLITS CAFÉ CHAMPAGNE BAR

I can't say I ever had the pleasure to enjoy a split of champagne at this long defunct champagne bar, nor did I ever fill up my tank with Texaco gas at this location. This sign was stuccoed over—a common death for a fading ad—shortly after I took this shot. This sign and service station presided over the busiest approach to the Holland Tunnel, the best route out of town when going to Jersey City, for decades. Gas filling stations have slowly begun to disappear in Manhattan. If you are low on gas, fill up before driving over a bridge or through a tunnel to get to the Big Apple. The filling stations here are few and far between, and there aren't any Texaco filling stations left in the New York City tri-state area.

Today on this same corner is built the most acutely sharp, triangular, five-story glass and black brick apartment building with a roof deck I have ever seen. Although a Greenwich Village apartment is a desirable location in the city, this particular corner is one of the noisiest and busiest. I shot this while coming out of class at SUNY Empire State College—Manhattan location—which used to be housed diagonally across from this ghost gas station.

Buy Texaco/Splits Café Champagne Bar—Seventh Avenue South, New York City. Taken June 1998. Ad circa 1960s.

Fading Light

Today, advertising signs in New York grace towering buildings that block out the light and display the names of Duane Reed and McDonald's, when, in former times, outdoor signs were for products like Omega Oil for "weak backs" and GiGi Young Originals from Lombardy Dresses. We've learned of these long obsolete ads because Frank Jump took time to notice them. My connection to Frank resulted from two tectonic shifts in technology: the first in the late nineteenth century, when electricity transformed our cities with light, and the second at the birth of the twenty-first century, when blogging unexpectedly emerged from the blossoming of the Internet. My blog, *Julian's Name*, and Frank's curiosity of this industry would enable him to find my story about my great-great-grandfather O.J. Gude, whose signs were among the first captured by Jump throughout his early photo documentation of New York City.

Oscar James Gude started his outdoor advertising firm, the O.J. Gude Co., in 1878 in Brooklyn with just $100 in capital. O.J. went on to pioneer the first use of the electric light bulb on a billboard in May 1892—just thirteen years after Thomas Edison invented the light bulb. But it wasn't just the lights that attracted advertisers like H.J. Heinz; it was the signs' movement. The electric sign's animation was made possible by tabulating machines that would go on to make International Business Machines a three-letter acronym in households around the world. O.J. used this nascent computing technology to precisely switch individual bulbs off and on, creating moving lightscapes. These lightscapes are what gave Broadway its name—the Great White Way—the dazzling and dancing white light cast from light bulbs in O.J.'s advertising "spectaculars" on Times Square. These were so novel and foreign in their day that in Theodore Dreiser's *Sister Carrie*, he called them "fire signs." Throughout its history, The O.J. Gude Sign Company of New York would produce over ten thousand painted wall ads and billboards around the United States.

Like most American success stories, O.J. came from humble immigrant beginnings. The son of a tailor from Hanover, Germany, who died when O.J. was fourteen, he went to work to support his mother and five young siblings. By the early twentieth century he had become a multimillionaire. O.J. made his money not only with his legendary spectaculars but also with ordinary painted and paper billboards. It is the hand-painted signs that have survived to be captured and chronicled by Frank, while the far more dazzling electric spectaculars of today's Times Square are lost forever.

Which brings me to discuss Frank's favorite photo of an O.J. Gude sign, M. Rappoport's Music Store, uncovered during building demolition. The ad features an early phonograph and record, along with the still famous RCA Victor Dog Nipper, who listens, head cocked, to "his master's voice" coming from the horn-shaped speaker. I can picture Frank looking at the sign and wondering about the music store and the people inside browsing through the newly invented gramophone recordings and marveling at their new playback devices.

I'm sure Frank wasn't aware of O.J.'s humble beginnings at the time he took this shot, or that later in O.J.'s life, after becoming successful, he turned away business from a fellow innovator who had recently developed a new way of mass producing cars that would prove far more important to the world than O.J.'s own use of light bulbs in signs. According to family lore, O.J. refused business from Henry Ford because Mr. Ford had "grease on his hands," and therefore, he thought that Ford would never be successful. Like many Victorians, O.J. valued appearances, saying that if down to his last twenty-five cents he would have chosen a shave over a meal because it could increase his chances of success. For all of O.J.'s business acumen, our family have passed down stories and letters that chronicle the many personal mistakes typical of this *nouveau riche*, including spoiling his children to the point that many of them

were unable to hold a job or attain even a piece of their father's business success, much less a life well lived.

Ironically, I ended up in the advertising business, not because O.J.'s business was passed down through generations but by accident. The O.J. Gude Co. of New York was sold off in the '20s; it didn't even live long enough to be passed down to O.J.'s children. As for myself, I had dreams of being involved with computer technology. In the late 1980s, I "went west," bound for Silicon Valley in an '85 Saab loaded full of clothes and dreams. But while searching for tech jobs in the *San Jose Mercury* classifieds, a position for a Yellow Pages advertising rep caught my eye. Before I could interview for any of my dream tech companies, I received a job offer making more money than I could imagine. Dreams of O.J.'s advertising riches swirled in my head.

Years later, I found a way to join the family trade of advertising with my love of technology by helping Yellow Pages, and later a traditional newspaper company, transition to online advertising. Soon, I was publishing my first personal blog, which eventually led me to form my own digital advertising and design company. When I wrote an article about O.J., it provided the connection to the old signs that Frank was capturing with his 35mm SLR. In a recent telephone conversation, Frank and I discussed how future generations might discover the wall art of people from earlier times since so much of our work has become digitized. We also discussed the fragility of our digitally stored world. Will much of it be forgotten on old computer servers and hard drives or just simply be victim of binary decay or obsolescence? Will these digital archives become the modern equivalent of finding a roll of undeveloped film in an attic trunk?

O.J. left behind work that vanishes from surfaces left from his time in a way that only has significance to us with the benefit of hindsight. These monumental forms of commercial art—O.J.'s advertising legacy—have a finite shelf life, and with the passage of time, they have become transformed. The transformation continues when contemporary visual images are captured by a camera, further extending the lives of these fading relics, giving them resonance in past, present and future time (an invisible abstraction). Long after we are gone, perhaps future generations will unearth these photographic images, not unlike the domestic wall art of Pompeii preserved beneath the volcanic ash of Vesuvius, and view them with the same sense of wonder and curiosity as the photographer who first produced this body of work, the Fading Ad Campaign—giving insight into the life of an artist who documented the work of past artisans. I have learned many things about my great-great-grandfather's work because of Frank's archive. His fading ads provided a bridge for me to link my life with my family history, along with a new appreciation of their place in time. I hope these images put a smile on your face, as they have for me.

Julian Seery Gude
Great-great-grandson of O.J. Gude

M. RAPPOPOR
MUSIC STORE

4109
Jamaica Ave.
near _____
Woodhaven Ave.

Victor

HIS MASTERS VOICE

The

Music and
Entertainment

M. Rappoport's Music Store

4109 Jamaica Avenue near Woodhaven Avenue.

This image depicts both opulence and obsolescence. The M. Rappoport's Music store ad is one of the most elaborate and beautifully colored painted ads of the Borough of Queens and was created by the O.J. Gude Company of New York. According to Gude's great-great-grandson Julian Seery Gude, "O.J. made his mark in a time of great change, where modern technological advances were having life changing impacts on people and societies the world round."[168] Prominently featured on this mural ad are the "victrola" and the flat disk phonograph, both examples of the most technologically advanced medium for playing sound recordings in its day.

In 1901, the Victor Phonograph Company sold its portable Victor for roughly $3. The Monarch Deluxe pictured in this ad sold for $60, an equivalent to $1,200 in today's economy.[169] Even today, these machines can be bought at flea markets and antique shops all over America for a couple of hundred dollars at most. Millions of brittle gramophone records (made of 25 percent shellac, powdered slate, cotton fibers and wax lubricant)[170] still are piled heavily in attics, bookshelves and warehouses across America and around the world. In 1939, the first flexible and "unbreakable" vinyl record for 78 rpm playback was introduced. Within forty years, the medium advertised on this mural became obsolete, replaced by the vinyl long-playing record that was played at 33.33 rpm.

If you think about the span of time that gramophone recordings were in vogue and compare them to the more recent compact disc, perhaps the former were longer-lived. Most people today download their music onto a computer and transfer the digital file (an AIFF, which is uncompressed, or an MP3, which is compressed), which is essentially an unfathomably long string of zeros and ones, to a digital recording device or MP3 player. Avid music listeners used to need wall space to store their recordings, and now we need disk space.

In the '60s, I loved the way a 45 felt in my hand, thick and thin between my index finger and thumb. Back in the 1970s, I could not wait to buy an LP so I could handle the cover to read the lyrics and ogle over the cover art. The tactile and visual pleasure of playing music today is gone.

The M. Rappoport's Music ad was revealed briefly while building a pharmacy. One day I took Vincenzo's niece Concetta around with me in search of signs.[171] When we busted into this construction site, the neighbors around this construction pit started coming out into their backyards to talk about this sign with me. Some people were confused as to how the sign "got there." Others were happy I was there

to document it. Although it was only exposed for a couple of months in the summer of '97, the sign looks from its quality that it had not seen the light of day for a very long time in the first place. The expansion of that section of Woodhaven along Jamaica Avenue went at a staggering pace. By the time the first box of replacement needles was used up for one of these Monarch Deluxe players, the adjacent building had already broken ground for construction. By the time the wall dog who painted this ad completed it, innovations were

speeding toward the electronic recording.

M. Rappoport's Music Store may be gone, but the ad still lurks silently behind a boxy, late 1990s Rite Aid Pharmacy construction. Given time, perhaps this corporation will cease to exist and the functionality for this building will also grow obsolete. Who knows, twenty years from now the neighbors of 89th and 90th Streets may come out of their back doors to stand on their backyard porches to ponder the arrival of this messenger from the past once again.

42ND STREET/THE WORLD'S GREATEST MOVIE CENTER/BICKFORD'S

Little nifties from the fifties,
Innocent and sweet.
Sexy ladies from the eighties,
Who are indiscrete oh!
—Al Dubin, "42nd Street"

The former Selwyn Office Building was scheduled to be demolished in the spring of 1998. It was being used as a visitors' center until it suddenly collapsed on December 30, 1997. The building's historic façade was to be incorporated into the New 42nd Street

Studio building. The Selwyn Theatre was also going to be demolished and rebuilt as the American Airlines Theatre where the Roundabout Theatre Company now resides. According to the Buena Vista University (Iowa) website, Edgar and Arch Selwyn opened the Selwyn Theatre in 1918 at the height of 42nd Street's hustle and bustle. Designed by theatre architect George Keister, the Selwyn was built in the Italian Renaissance style,

"decorated in gold and blue with large murals adorning the walls," and had seating for over one thousand people with two levels of box seats.[172]

Next door was a shuttered, closed Bickford's. Almost like a domino effect, the entire block has been transformed since this picture was taken. Anyone coming out of a fourteen-year coma would not be able to recognize 42nd Street today. In the 1970s and 1980s, the kinds of films that played in

these theatres were not what one would call family-oriented films. What was once a dicey, somewhat seedy and always challenging street to walk down is now a Disney ride. This is the block where I saw my first adult film and where I bought my first fake ID at age fourteen. My father finally gave it back to me last year after confiscating it in 1974. The excitement of 42nd Street is still there, but the sleaze has been completely whitewashed.

The sign reads "Cooped up? Feelin' low? Enjoy a movie today." Although many of the original movie theatres have been torn down, rebuilt or expanded, the block can still boast to having close to forty movie screens between the AMC Theatres–Empire 25 and Regal Cinemas E-Walk Stadium. A majority of this block's transformation took

place within five years from November 1995, when all adult theatres on the north side of 42nd Street were closed down, to July 2000, when the American Airlines Theatre opened its doors.[173]

Prior to the 1970s, as evidenced from this photograph, this was a place where you could sit at a cafeteria counter for breakfast, lunch or dinner and not spend an arm and a leg. The business just to the right of this ad was a Bickford's Restaurant, which can be seen written on the ceramic tiled marquis. David W. Dunlap writes the following about Bickford's:

If you lived in New York anytime from the 1930's through the 1960's, chances are you knew Bickford's. They were up and down Broadway, on Fordham Road and the Grand Concourse in the Bronx, Nostrand Avenue and Fulton Street in Brooklyn, Main Street and Jamaica Avenue in Queens.

"Breakfast at Bickford's is an old New York custom," a 1964 guidebook said. "In these centrally located, speedy-service, modestly-priced restaurants a torrent of traffic is sustained for a generous span

of hours with patrons who live so many different lives on so many different shifts."

To say the least. The best minds of Allen Ginsberg's generation "sank all night in submarine light of Bickford's," he wrote in "Howl." The Beat Generation muse, Herbert Huncke, practically inhabited the Bickford's on West 42nd Street. Walker Evans photographed Bickford's customers, and Andy Warhol rhapsodized about Bickford's waitresses. Bickford's make its way into the work of writers as diverse as Woody Allen and William Styron.[174]

"Death (being edged to the doorway): Where's a good hotel? What am I talking about hotel, I got no money. I'll go sit in Bickford's. (He picks up the News)."
—Getting Even, Woody Allen

"How vividly there still lingers on my palate the suety aftertaste of the Salisbury steak at Bickford's, or Riker's western omelette, in which one night, nearly swooning, I found a greenish, almost incorporeal feather and a tiny embryonic beak."
—Sophie's Choice, William Styron

WABC MUSIC RADIO 77

Ron Lundy, Harry Harrison, Cousin Brucie—these were the most influential voices of my childhood. These men were the DJs of my era. My fondest memories were those sunny days when Mom said, "Pack up a pail and shovel, we're goin' to the beach. And don't forget the transistor radio!" The sounds of Motown filled the salty air of the Rockaways. And the Beatles, Beach Boys and all those fabulous hits we now call classic oldies flew over the radio waves and floated above the surf. I can still hear the roar of the rollercoaster of Rockaway's Playland. Maybe I'm just getting old, but they don't make 'em like that anymore.

ODEON THEATRE

In an interview with Harlemite and Manhattan borough historian Celedonia "Cal" Jones, he said he remembered sneaking into the Odeon in the late 1930s to watch movies as a child. Cal, who lived two or three blocks north of the Odeon, said, "When you go shopping for theatres to sneak into, you perfected your talents on the local theatres. We had it down pretty pat." Cal recounted, "One of us snuck in and he'd come around and crack the door and the rest of us would crawl upstairs." Sometimes he would "back into the theatre," which is the remarkable talent of walking backward while people were exiting. Cal also remembers that the Odeon

used to give out sets of jelly glasses to the first hundred paying customers who got in the theatre or some other kind of promotional gift. Usually the Odeon showed a double feature but not first-run films. "After it hit downtown, it would work its way uptown, so for the area, they were first runs." Cal's buddy Sonny Neal remembered the newsreels between the films. Sonny said they would show the black newsreels after the general newsreels, like the clips about the all-black troops during World War II. Cal remembers he had heard the theatre once had live vaudeville performances, but by the time he was "coming up" in Harlem, during its renaissance, the Odeon was a straight movie house.

In a letter written by the New York City Landmarks Preservation Committee to restore the Apollo Theatre (formerly known as the Hurtig & Seaman's New Burlesque Theatre), the following information about the Odeon Theatre was provided:

Brecher and Schiffman were white businessmen who played a major role in the history of Harlem's entertainment industry as owner-operators of a number of Harlem's leading theatres featuring black entertainers. Brecher was owner of several Broadway and Harlem clubs and theatres, while Schiffman was a theatre operator and motion picture distributor. They first became business partners in 1920, converting the Odeon Theatre (1910, Van Buren & Lavelle, 256 West 145th Street) to show motion pictures.[175]

Many of the old theatres and movie houses had elaborate organs that were played in between vaudeville acts or during films, which up to then were still silent films. There is an interesting connection between the owners of the Odeon and a young jazz organist by the name of Thomas Waller. While reading some selected passages from the book *Black and Blue: The Life and Lyrics of Andy Razaf* by Barry Singer,

required reading for a course at the Center for the Humanities at Washington University at St. Louis about the American poet and jazz lyricist Andy Razaf, I was happy to discover that his musical partner, twenty-year-old Thomas "Fats" Waller, was employed by Brecher and Schiffman.

Wildly unsuited to a wife who'd finally divorced her unreliable musician-husband in late 1923, and still sorely missing his late mother, young Waller reveled in the camaraderie of musicians, loving to jam with them, loving to drink with them. The orchestra rows surrounding his organ post at the Lincoln Theatre often were filled with musician friends drinking in Waller's astonishing keyboard talent, passing the bottle, laughing with him as he often provided outrageous musical accompaniment to the action onscreen. Willie "the Lion" Smith would later suggest that Waller's unsuspected, painful shyness was the cause of his early alcoholism. Everyone, including young Waller, loved the person he became boozed up. The drinking escalated rapidly.

In March 1925 Marie Downes, owner of the Lincoln Theatre, informed her organist that she had decided to sell

OPPOSITE, LEFT
WABC Music Radio 77—Harlem. Taken August 1999. Ad circa early 1970s.

OPPOSITE, RIGHT
Odeon Theatre—West 145th Street, Harlem. Taken August 1997. Sign circa 1920s.

the old film house to Frank Schiffman and his partner Leo Brecher—two white men, operators of the Odeon Theatre on 145th Street and both the Harlem Opera House and Loew's Seventh Avenue burlesque theatre on 124th Street, who were about to attempt an ambitious consolidation of black vaudeville entertainment in Harlem.

The news stung Waller, who viewed the Lincoln in much the same light as he did the revered memory of his late mother. Schiffman and Brecher, however, cordially brought the young keyboardist up to their offices, where they openly informed him of their plans to turn the Lincoln into a straight movie house while transferring the old theatre's successful vaudeville programming to the larger Lafayette, which, after undergoing continual policy reconfigurations over the previous few years, was for the moment a straight movie house presenting only sporadic stage shows. The two men then offered Waller the Lafayette organist's job for $50 a week (double his Lincoln Theatre salary), crowning the news with the information that if he accepted, Waller could expect to play a Robert Marston—

model organ at the Lafayette, the first grand organ to be found in Harlem.[176]

Cal Jones informed me that the Odeon is currently in use as St. Paul's Community Church. Since organ music is also common in church ritual and the seating capacity can afford a larger audience, it explains why so many of these old theatres in New York made the transition to becoming churches. On the New York City Chapter of the American Guild of Organists' website, some additional information was provided about the organ and the dramatic shift of tenor that occurred at the Odeon from the profane to the sacred. Established in 1947, St. Paul's Community Church was founded after a controversy within the African Methodist Episcopal Church. After the removal of the Reverend Hale B. Thompson as pastor of the Bethel AME Church, St. Paul's Community Church was formed and called upon Thompson to head their church. The former Odeon 145th Street Theatre, designed by Thomas W. Lamb and built in 1910, was purchased by this church group in 1952. The theatre's organ was originally built by M.P. Möller as Op. 3963 for the Mecca Temple

(now the City Center 55th Street Theatre) at 130 West 55th Street in 1924 and had "four manuals and 37 ranks." In 1955, Möller rebuilt this organ, providing "several new ranks and a new three-manual drawknob console."[177]

The movement from vaudeville theatres to movie houses and then to churches all came about due to the economic and demographic shifts in Harlem's population. Cal Jones remembers that in the 1920s, Harlem was undergoing rapid changes when whites were moving from Harlem to the suburbs. When a row of buildings on 135th Street was bought up by St. Philip's Episcopal (formerly the Free African Church of St. Philip), this "opened the floodgates" to African Americans moving to Harlem. Cal recounts his teachers in elementary school (the poet Countee Cullen was his English teacher) telling him that when they would show performers in black face on the films at the RKO Alhambra Theatre on 125th Street, people would pelt the screen with rotten eggs from the balcony, where the blacks were relegated to sit. The Odeon's building sign is yet another reminder of Harlem's rich and vibrant past.

Hardman Duo Player Piano

Twice the Fun.

The sounds of ragtime piano being played from a scratchy 78 rpm gramophone record constitute the perfect soundtrack to a documentary film about fading ads. So often when being presented images from the turn of the century, we watch silent films from a time that seems slightly sped up and out of sync as Model Ts dart around jerkily through crowded intersections filled with quickly paced pedestrians, or we gaze with nostalgia at the television as a camera pans slowly over a vintage sepia-tone albumen print of a 1900s Orchard Street scene in a style now called "The Ken Burns Effect" while listening to an old player piano roll churning out a popular piano tune from that day.

Before the advent of the gramophone record player, player pianos witnessed a dramatic rise in popularity in the late nineteenth century. There were several key players who led to the development and mass production of the player piano. Thaddeus Kochanny of the Chicago Chapter of the Automatic Musical Instrument Collectors' Association (AMICA) wrote the following synopsis about these developments:

In 1863, the Frenchman [Henri] Fourneaux invented the player piano. He called it, "Pianista," the first pneumatic piano mechanism, which was introduced at the Philadelphia Centennial Exhibition in 1876. In 1887, a year after [Edwin] Votey invented the Pianola; Edwin Welte [Welte-Mignon system] introduced the perforated paper roll in Germany. The perforated roll mechanism to make music was based on the Jacquard punch cards used to weave designs into cloth.[178]

Votey's Pianola is the player piano that became most popular in the United States. The technology was such that mass production of these costly instruments (about $250, today's equivalent of about $6,000)[179] made them readily available to those who could afford real-time acoustic piano music in their home or business. On the Pianola Institute's website, dedicated to the history of the pianola and Votey's achievements, it is explained that "the basic principal upon which Votey's system operated subsequently became the standard for virtually all roll operated piano playing systems." The Aeolian Corporation acquired the U.S. rights from Votey to market his piano player system from 1897 as the pianola and later became "the world's leading manufacturer of roll operated instruments." Votey's main achievement was melding the best of preexisting player piano designs, creating "an instrument that would enjoy mass market appeal for three decades."[180]

The brightest star of the piano roll production industry was Jean Lawrence Cook, an African American musician and arranger (and World War I veteran) who transcribed the first ragtime tunes in the early days of jazz. J. Lawrence Cook was to the music roll industry what Quincy Jones was to the modern recording industry. After

freelancing for several of the leading music roll companies, Cook was hired in May 1923 by the QRS Music Roll Company (later QRS Records). John Farrell, a contributor for a website called the Monrovia Sound Studio,[181] documented the following about Cook:

Cook was a musical chameleon—he could produce convincing keyboard impressions of Art Tatum, "Fats" Waller, Teddy Wilson, Erroll Garner and several other leading pianists of the day. However, a major part of his QRS career was spent producing arrangements of commercial pop songs, as required for the catalogue of a commercial roll producer, and it is to Cook's credit that his unique skill injected musicality into otherwise unexceptional material.[182]

At the height of the production of player pianos in the early 1920s, literally

hundreds of thousands of piano rolls were distributed across the United States and Europe. In a *Time* magazine article published on February 15, 1943, the pianola was remembered as such:

In the heyday of 1923, when 197,252 pianolas (more than 50% of all the pianos sold in the U.S.) were sold in a single year, the pianola industry hired the greatest pianists, such as Paderewski, to record their performances on perforated paper. It also hired such early jazzers as J. Lawrence Cook and Harlem's historic James P. Johnson. But as the pianola gave ground to the phonograph, the pianola industry could no longer afford to pay for personal recordings.[183]

With the advent of affordable radios and the crash of 1929 came the near annihilation of the player piano industry, as "uncounted thousands of these instruments were chopped up and used for fuel."[184] Throughout the Depression, largely due to the brilliance of J. Lawrence Cook, and with a new financier, Max Kortlander (himself an accomplished pianist), the QRS Company struggled to

maintain itself after a brief production stoppage. It is said that Cook's most celebrated arrangements occurred in the period between the 1940s and 1950s. The player piano industry witnessed its resurgence in the 1950s, with newer models of player pianos being produced by a handful of companies, one of which was the Hardman DUO.

An exciting innovation in piano design and engineering has led to the creation of the Hardman DUO, the amazing new player-piano developed and manufactured exclusively by Hardman, Peck & Co. Unveiled in the Spring of 1957, the DUO is actually two pianos in one. At once an incomparable Hardman Console famed for acoustical richness is changed from manual to a player-piano, ready to play any of the hundreds of melodies on music rolls—everything from classics to rock 'n roll.[185]

Professor Alan Wallace, also a jazz musician, contributed the following comments to the Monrovia Studios Website that were gleaned from the liner notes of a Mercury Records recording featuring Cook:

In 1959 Mercury Records released a 12-inch long-playing stereo record titled PIANO-ROLL ROCK'N ROLL. The record features 12 music rolls by J. Lawrence Cook. Guitar, string bass and drums accompany the numbers. Mercury SR 60083.

The liner notes on the reverse side of the record cover give no indication that Lawrence was involved in the actual recording. However, his music rolls, played on a Hardman Duo Player Piano, are in good company with accompanying musicians,

Milton Hinton, Tony Mottola, George Duvivier and Osie Johnson.

In the mid 1950's, the Hardman Piano Company, introduced the "Hardman Duo," an electrified player piano in a modern "console" case. The company slogan was "It's Twice The Fun when Your Piano is 2-in-1—See The Hardman Duo today!"[186]

J. Lawrence Cook produced over twenty thousand arrangements for the pianola within a mile from where this sign was photographed.

Cook's legacy is immortalized in countless sheets of perforated paper, now perhaps deteriorating in dusty attics or destroyed due to obsolescence. Even the vinyl recordings of his work (which were never reissued as CDs) are destined to decay. In an August 20, 2010 *Buffalo News* article entitled "The Day the Music Died," reporter Mark Sommer wrote, "When the last piano roll was manufactured at QRS Music Technologies in Buffalo, NY, The remark scribbled at the end of the production sheet said simply, 'End of era.'"[187]

CAMERA MART

This ad was also painted by the Mack Sign Company. Camera Mart was incorporated on July 16, 1948, and dissolved its corporation on April 15, 1991.[188] One of its most notable rental gigs was for the music documentary *Woodstock* in 1970. Other notable films include *Glengarry Glen Ross* (1992), *The Prince of Tides* (1991), *Green Card* (1990), *New York Stories* (1989), *Big* (1988), *Sophie's Choice* (1982), *Kramer vs. Kramer* (1979) and *Pumping Iron* (1970).[189]

WE MAKE VIDEO EASIER
Whether you're new to video or not, we at Camera Mart can help. With the most comprehensive line of video equipment. For every type of industrial, educational or medical production. Camera, recorders, monitors, receivers, production and editing systems. For sale, rent or long-term lease.

But equipment is just the half of it. The other half is our people. Knowledgeable,

dedicated professionals who make sure you get the right components or system for any application. Factory-trained people who inspect and test everything and provide the best service in the business.

If you're looking for the answer to your video equipment needs, look no further than Camera Mart. It's that easy! Send for our video catalogue today.
—ad in the November 1980 issue of Videography[190]

Camera Mart—Tenth Avenue and 456 West 55th Street, New York City. Taken August 1999. Ad circa 1960s.

Hotels,
Speakeasies
and Saunas

Hotel Irvin

From 2.50 up

Grutchfield wrote that the Hotel Irvin for Women was named for Mary M. Irvin, president of the group that worked for years to establish a women's residence. As early as 1916, the organization planned a hotel "where self-supporting girls and women with small incomes could be accommodated comfortably and well at little cost."[191] By 1924, the organization had "managed to acquire the land and begin construction" at 308 West 30th Street. Asher Mayer (president) and Charles H. Strong (treasurer) opened the hotel in 1925 "for exclusive occupany by business women [with apartments] arranged in small flexible units with facilities for self-housekeeping [and rents] adjusted on a basis to meet the big demand that exists for this type of housing."[192] According to Grutchfield, the Irvin seemed to drop the women-only policy in the 1940s and went out of business by the mid-1950s.[193] This sign has been well documented by other fading ad enthusiasts on the Internet on photo-sharing sites like Flickr. I seemed lucky to find it with a rainbow flag waving atop.

Henry Hudson Hotel

In 1998, Ian Schrager, former Studio 54 partner and hotelier (Royalton Hotel), made it known that he was going to renovate the old Henry Hudson Hotel at 353 West 57th Street and reopen it as an affordable boutique hotel by 2000. Originally built about 1929 and financed by Anne Morgan, the daughter of the financier J.P. Morgan, it was to serve as the American Women's Association clubhouse and also function as a residence for young New York City women. According to Christopher Gray of the *New York Times*, Morgan "used her huge inheritance to advance causes of social justice among her crowd of socially advantaged women."[194]

PREVIOUS PAGES
Hotel Irvin—West 30th Street and Eighth Avenue, Midtown, New York City. Taken August 1998.

OPPOSITE
Henry Hudson Hotel—West Side Highway, New York City. Taken June 1998. Ad circa 1950s.

According to Gray, the clubhouse did pretty well considering it was built around the year of the stock market crash, but by 1941, it was succumbing to bankruptcy, so the savvy Ms. Morgan decided to convert the clubhouse into a hotel for both men and women and call it the Henry Hudson. Gray stated that during the hotel's grand opening, "an 11-year-old Dutch girl smashed a bottle of Dutch milk against the doorway." Gray reported that the United Nations Security Council met in the hotel in 1946. It was later the headquarters of WNET, New York City's local public television station, from where the *MacNeil/Lehrer NewsHour* was broadcast, but WNET moved after the recent renovation by Schrager to its new location on West 33rd Street. Gray also commented, "As for the American Woman's Association, it withered and was defunct by 1980, and its cornerstone—with its predictions for the future—sits undisturbed."[195]

YOUNG & SCHMUCK

Fine Wines, Liquors and Cigars—Pool & Billiard Parlor

On August 27, 2000, Daniel B. Schneider of the *New York Times* reported on this five-story tenement building at 772 Eighth Avenue, at Hell's Kitchen's eastern border, which, in its time was "a broad-shouldered factory and tenement district that by the late 19th century was one of the city's grittier slums," populated by a mostly Irish demographic that included Scots, Germans and African Americans. In Schneider's interview with the architectural historian and *New York Times* writer Christopher Gray, it was revealed that:

Fred Schmuck was the original owner of the building, which was built in 1873. The wide, handsome tenements now being demolished to the north were built in 1897; the "Young & Schmuck" sign was no doubt painted during this 24-year period, when pool halls were becoming popular around the city. Mr. Gray added, however, that census records and city directories during these years do not show a Young or a Schmuck at the address, or associated with a billiard parlor.

Mr. Gray also said newspaper reports beginning *in the 1890's record many police raids of liquor, gambling and prostitution dens in the area, but Young & Schmuck's billiard parlor was not mentioned. Further research is called for.*

As recently as last year, 772 Eighth Avenue retained an astonishingly unaltered, turn-of-the-century wooden storefront, beneath layer upon layer of chipped and peeling paint.[196]

According to James T. Young of Gray, Tennessee, in a telephone interview on July 22, 2011, his great-grandfather,

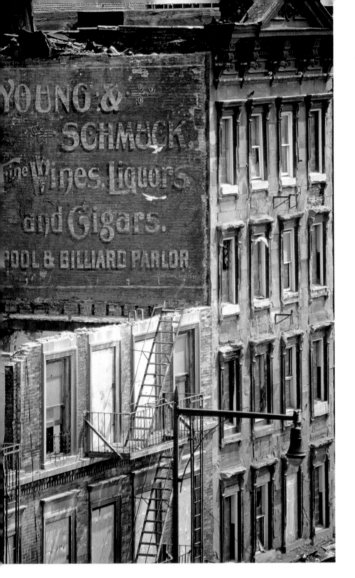

Young & Schmuck—Eighth Avenue and 47th Street. Taken September 2000.

In addition to running the family business, Pop Young was also in real estate and the coal-supplying business, as well as being "a barman, carpenter and Union President the 1900s in New York City and Florida." On James T. Young's genealogy page, he shares the following anecdotes about his great-grandfather as told by his grandmother, Emma Bartko, who was born on March 17, 1872, near Miskolc, Hungary, and immigrated to New York City in 1885. Bartko claimed Young

was known to own a racehorse at old Aqueduct in NY. Him being voted out of office as Union president during the Depression was probably part due to this horse. He originated in New York City's "Kitchen"; only outsiders called it "Hell's Kitchen." His past position as a Labor man offered an opportunity to his grandson Jimmy to choose almost any trade Union job including working as a "Checker" on the "Docks."

When he was dying in a Catholic hospital he became a Catholic. His son (my father) at the church services said "He always was a gambling man, we're lucky

James T. "Pop" Young, was born in 1869 in the United States and at age four returned to Scotland to be raised by his aunt. In recounting his great-grandfather's saga, Young said he had returned to the United States divorced from his first wife Ann Lowe, with whom he had three children. Young said that "his great-great grandfather was also in an early billiard parlor and gin joint business in 'The Kitchen' in the 1890's or thereabouts in New York City."

he wasn't dying in a Jewish hospital, else we might be standing with Yarmulke's on and in a Synagogue." His wife was less gracious, who as a Catholic believed he was entitled an instant trip to heaven, having just been baptized. "I can't believe GOD is letting that SOB get directly into heaven

after the life he led, leaving me, drinking, gambling and what ever else!" He sure doesn't deserve it. The Mass was even funnier…his Scot Rite Mason friends stood outside the Church with Masonic salutes wondering how the Catholics had won him over?[197]

James T. "Pop" Young died on January 16, 1951, in New York City and was buried on January 19, 1951, in Evergreen Cemetery in Brooklyn (Burial #366578). Emma Bartko died in August 1974 in a nursing home in Queens and was buried in Maple Grove Cemetery in Queens.

MOUNT MORRIS BATHS—STEAM & TURKISH

LEhigh 4-9004

According to Aviva Stampfer, a writer on the Place Matters website, a joint project of City Lore and the New York Municipal Art Society, the Mount Morris Baths

was founded in 1898 by a group of Jewish doctors, when Turkish (hot air) baths were an important part of the religious and social traditions of Eastern European Jews. The doctors lived on the upper floors, using the basement as a professional spa. In the 1920s, Finnish immigrant Hugo Koivenon bought the baths and incorporated Finnish features such as "needle showers" and vitea treatments. East Harlem

residents (especially those living in the neighborhood's many cold water flats) came for the sauna, steambath and therapeutic pool.[198]

This was the sign to the Mount Morris Baths as you looked down the stairs at its entrance on the basement level, below the street and somewhat out of view of the sidewalk passersby. The plastic illuminated sign that hung high up over its entrance and said "Turkish Baths—Mt. Morris— Men Only" harkened back to a time when there weren't many legal challenges based on gender discrimination for entering a public place as this. As you walked in, there were

safe-sex brochures and free condoms available, although the signs prohibiting explicit sex on the premises juxtaposed to the posters about safe sex seemed contradictory. The place had a musty smell, and I imagine that there were still some of the original water

OPPOSITE
Mount Morris Baths—Steam & Turkish—Harlem. Taken April 1997. Sign circa 1950s.

molecules circulating in the fetid, steamy mist since its maiden *shvitz* of 1898.

In a January 2003 article for the *New York Times*, journalist Alan Feuer provided the following more recent historical context about this bathhouse:

Twenty years ago, at the height of the AIDS epidemic, the gay bathhouse scene was nearly run out of town when state officials enacted a raft of laws banning many homosexual gathering places. The New St. Marks Baths in the East Village, for example, was shut in 1985 by the City Department of Health and was replaced nine years later by a video rental store.

The Mount Morris bathhouse, the only one in the city that caters to gay blacks, has been operating continuously since 1893 and survived the crackdown essentially for two reasons. First, it is far from the city's gay meccas, on a quiet, unassuming block of Madison Avenue at East 125th Street, across the street from the offices of the Rev. Al Sharpton. Second, it has matured through the years, remaining a place to meet

new people and enjoy a steam, but with the reality of the city health code's prohibition on open sex.[199]

Apparently, the owner at the time, Walter Fitzer, a retired mechanical engineer and volunteer firefighter from Lynbrook, New York, seemed "an unlikely candidate [to Feuer] to be running a bathhouse known for attracting gay black men." Notwithstanding, it was my experience growing up gay in New York City that most of the bars and bathhouses were owned by straight, white men. Fitzer told Feuer in his interview, "'I always tell the clients, 'If I can't bring my wife down here, it isn't right.'" Having been a patron of this establishment in the late 1980s when I was living in Harlem before it was destroyed by what the city called "urban renewal," I couldn't imagine anyone bringing their wife to Mount Morris. It was by no means a Plato's Retreat, which was a sex club that opened in 1977 in the basement of the Ansonia Hotel that did cater to a more "ecumenical" crowd. One of my favorite understatements from Fitzer in this interview is:

"Bathhouses have been gay since the days of the Greeks. It's no big secret."[200]

According to Feuer, Fitzer also claimed, "Harlem royalty like Joe Louis and Sam Cooke used to sweat here years ago, and it is nothing to see French tourists, straight businessmen and Hasidic Jews perspiring in the steam room, side by side."

On the Place Matters website, Stampfer also presented the following:

Mount Morris attracted a mixed clientele that included area residents and patients of nearby North General Hospital. Mount Morris became known as well for its emphasis on sex education, providing condoms, lubricant, and brochures, and also hiring an education director who held a lecture series five nights a week on topics of interest to gay men, and ran a popular G.E.D. program.[201]

Despite the discrepancies in the year this *mikva* or ritual Jewish bath was founded, for at least seventy of the over one hundred years this establishment was operating, it was frequented chiefly by gay African American men. Many people, like myself, wondered why this sauna was overlooked for nearly a decade when gay bathhouses were systematically closed during the '80s by the New York City Department of Health in its hasty response to the AIDS crisis. And why had it survived unscathed? Didn't New York City health commissioner Stephen Joseph and the Koch administration care enough about *black* male homosexuals? I don't believe it was left open out of any consideration by Koch for the services Mount Morris provided. For the most part, the city was totally unprepared for the AIDS crisis when it hit with a vengeance.[202]

I remember challenging Koch in August 1987 during his obligatory momentary appearance at the New York City chapter of Parents of Gays annual awards dinner when I asked him why there wasn't a public service campaign on safe sex aimed at New York City's LGBT community, as there was in San Francisco. Koch's typical flippant response was, "Oh, the gays here know what to do." So I began chanting, "You're full of shit" and was joined by my friend Andy Humm and others until Koch stormed out of the banquet hall. Urban legend has it that later that evening on the news, it was

said that Koch collapsed in Chinatown after overeating at one of his favorite restaurants.

In a recent telephone conversation with my longtime friend and journalist Andy Humm (*Gay City News*), he commented to me that it was fortuitous that Mount Morris had remained open as long as it did after the bathhouse closings since it provided much-needed services to its community. In addition, the pioneering and exemplary work of the Minority AIDS Task Force (1985), Harlem United (1988) and other grass-roots community organizations that targeted black and Latino populations that weren't publicly gay helped an ailing community that was for the most part in denial. Sadly, I was alerted by e-mails through my website of the sauna's closing in 2003 and wondered why there wasn't the same uproar in the gay community as there was over the closing of the Wall Street Sauna in February 2004. Of course, south of 110th Street there were private AIDS organizations like Gay Men's Health Crisis (1981) and the AIDS Resource Center (Bailey House, 1983) that had been mobilized since the onset of the epidemic and provided services initially for

self-identified gay men, usually white, with regard to education about AIDS prevention, medical and financial counseling and advocacy.

Humm also reminded me that in the early days of ACT UP, there were two camps with totally divergent ideologies: one, those who wanted to aid the City of New York in creating guidelines for establishments where public sex was a potential in an attempt to keep them open; and two, those who wanted no restrictions at all on public spaces because any limitations would be an infringement of their personal freedoms. Ultimately, both camps lost the battle because many of these sex establishments that provided the only reliable sources of HIV/AIDS prevention materials were closed in spite of their attempts to work with the failures of the Koch administration. Today, I have heard, the sex clubs are opening up again and are filled with young people who did not experience the horror of disease, loss and grief as we did as young people living through the height of the AIDS epidemic in the '80s and '90s. Remember, folks—the AIDS crisis is not over!

Rosario Dawson and Her Uncle Frank

Born and raised in NYC, Rosario began her film career by accident when she was cast off the street to act in the 1995 indie production "Kids." The film propelled Rosario in the acting world. She went on to attend the Lee Strasberg Theater Institute and soon after started appearing in movies such as "He Got Game," "Josie and the Pussycats," "Men in Black II," "The Adventures of Pluto Nash," "25ᵗʰ Hour," "Alexander," and most recently "Sin City" and "RENT."

At the age of 16, while in high school, Rosario decided to live with Uncle Frank and partner Vincenzo Aiosa. Frank is photographer/composer…and a NYC Public School Teacher. Rosario has great memories of living with Frank and Vincenzo, who—by the way—got married in Toronto in 2004. Frank has been a great influence in her life and she treasures their relationship tremendously.[203]

Why This Campaign is So Important: It is estimated that one in 4 families includes someone that is gay, lesbian, bisexual, or transgendered. 69% of GLBT youth report experiencing some form of harassment or violence, with 46% reporting verbal harassment, 36% reporting sexual harassment, 12% reporting physical harassment, and 6% reporting physical assault.

Gay and lesbian youths are two to three times more likely to commit suicide than other youths. Of 1.3 million homeless children on America's streets, 500,000 are thought to be GLBT kids thrown out by their parents.

How This Campaign Came About: These facts could not be ignored any longer. So in 2002, PFLAG NY took the lead in developing an awareness campaign to get the word out about the PFLAG organization to parents, families, teachers, clergy, politicians, GLBT people, and the general public. The goal was to reach people who would most benefit from PFLAG's services and, ultimately, to increase acceptance, reduce bigotry, and change hearts and minds.

PFLAG NY recruited talented individuals from various fields (advertising, PR, law, media) to work pro bono on the awareness effort, which became known as the "Stay Close" campaign. After three years in the making, PFLAG NY launched "Stay Close" featuring straight celebrities with their gay relatives. The message is simple: Stay Close to your loved ones because relationships are too precious to lose.[204]

I was so grateful when Rosa took the time to participate in this incredibly important campaign while she was in production for the film *Rent*, for which she played an HIV-positive young woman named Mimi. Rosa also knew how important this organization was to my mother, Willy. For over twenty-one years, Willy Jump helped parents cope with learning about their LGBT children at the NYC chapter of PFLAG (Parents, Families and Friends of Lesbians and Gays) alongside her dear friends Amy and Dick Ashworth. After marching with me in the first LGBT March on Washington in 1979 and meeting the Ashworths for the first time, my mom vowed to march with me in New York City, which she did proudly behind the PFLAG banner in the NYC LGBT Pride Parade for over twenty years since 1980.

The morning of the event in New York City in 1980—which traditionally took place on the last Sunday in June to commemorate the Stonewall Inn riots of 1969—I told my mom to meet me on the corner of Bedford and Christopher Streets an hour before the march was to begin its "illegal lurch" uptown toward Central Park, thinking it wouldn't be that crowded yet. (I'm not sure when the first legally obtained permit for the march was, but it was a *march* long before it became a *parade*.)

So here I am desperately looking for my mom, peering over the throngs of leather queens, drag queens, dykes on bikes and twinks, screaming, "MOM! MOM!" while perched on a nearby lamppost. Almost immediately, this dashing older gentleman with an impish *diastemaed* smile came up to me and tugged my pant leg while shouting at me over the din in his incredibly coarse voice that seemed incongruous to his appearance. "You really aren't looking for your *MOM*, but some big queen you call MOM—right?" "No," I said, slowly realizing to whom I was responding. "I really *am* looking for my mom."

Slowly putting his fingernail up to his mouth to hide his incredulity, he began sputtering like a typewriter on steroids in a rapid-fire breathy dragon voice: "OH MY GOD! If my mother would just even *acknowledge* my being gay, let alone come *marching* with me! COME MARCHING WITH ME? I could die right now a happy drag queen. Do you know how lucky you are? I have to meet this WOMAN! MOM! MOM! MOM!"

And almost as soon as he began calling, my mother happily appeared, exclaiming, "Hi, Frankie. Who is your friend?" I told her that this was the inimitable Harvey Fierstein. "Points! Points! You are scoring here," Harvey raspily whispered. "And *this* is my mother, Willy Jump," I proudly exclaimed. Harvey grabbed my mother around the neck and planted a wet one on her cheek.

Not surprisingly, the two of them would run into each other for the next decade at LGBT events on panel discussions. I ran into Harvey repeatedly over the years, from book signings to random rides on the subway while he was going to the theatre to perform *Torch Song* to spotting him on parade floats—always with a warm, gravelly greeting, "How's your mother?"

Needless to say, the '80s were a very difficult time for parents of gay men in the organization, particularly the Ashworths, who lost two sons to AIDS. My continued wish is that through the efforts of my mom, my niece, parents and friends of the LGBT community across the country, and brilliantly audacious public figures like Harvey Fierstein, this cause doesn't become just another fading ad campaign.

Prostheses
and
Undertaker

POMEROY TRUSSES, ELASTIC STOCKINGS, ABDOMINAL BELTS, ARTIFICIAL LEGS

The history of this company was revealed to me through its advertising in various medical journals and business directories from 1880 to 1941. Arthur C. Pomeroy claimed he would "attend personally to the careful adjustment and adaptation to each case o[f] his specialties in Trusses." These products were offered in a print advertisement in the 1880 *Proceedings of the Medical Society of the County of Kings*, locating the business at 746 Broadway on the corner of Astor Place:

POMEROY'S TRUSSES. The "Finger Pad," The "Water Pad," The "Frame Trusses," The "Jointed Spring Trusses," The "Elastic Rupture Belt," &c. Dr. Richardson's Clavicle and Let Splints, Elastic Stockings, Knee Caps, Belts, &c., Crutches, Shoulder Braces, Suspensories, Abdominal Supporters, Club Foot Shoes, Leg Braces, and other Surgical Appliances.

Ladies may avail themselves of the services of a skillful and experienced female attendant, with Mr. Pomeroy's advice and aid, in the selection and preparation of such appliances as may be required…Instruments for prolapsus ani, Trusses for inguinal and umbilical hernia of infants, and other surgical appliances. COMMON TRUSSES FITTED AT LOW PRICES[205]

Prolapsus ani. Ouch. Pomeroy offered quite an impressive list of prosthetic devices and services to aid the troubled body, with special consideration for female patients. Pomeroy placed another ad in the *Pennsylvania Medical Journal* 9, no. 2, published by the Medical Society of the State of Pennsylvania from 1905 to 1906. By 1906, Pomeroy had moved his office location to 17 Union Square and had opened a second office at 414 Fulton Street in Brooklyn. In this ad, Pomeroy claimed: "Our Specialty is the fitting of trusses by the Frame method. We guarantee, with this truss, to retain securely and comfortably the hernia of any person referred to us. Difficult cases that have been considered unholdable, are especially solicited. We have such coming to us from all parts of the country, and invariably give them complete satisfaction."[206]

By 1910, the Pomeroy "Frame" Truss franchise had opened offices throughout the Tri-State area. Several locations in the New York City area were opened to service the needs of an ailing and rapidly growing population. A medical directory from 1910 revealed the following information about the company's founding:

ARTHUR C. POMEROY, Pres. & Treas. HENRY M. DEAN. Sec.
Established 1867—
Incorporated 1875
Pomeroy Company 34 EAST 23d STREET (Bet. B'way & 4th Ave.) Telephone, 6881 Gramercy
330 LENOX Ave., Near 126th Street Telephone, 2388 Harlem

*208 LIVINGSTON
STREET, BROOKLYN
825 BROAD STREET,
NEWARK, N.J. Telephone,
2433 Market*

*The Pomeroy Frame
Truss FOR HERNIA
SUPPORTING BELTS
MADE, TO FIT…Skillful
and experienced women
will attend ladies at our
application rooms, or, if the
physician so requests, at their
residences.*[207]

Again, it is advertised that
female specialists would attend
to female patients. Also, the
house call is offered as an
available option for services.
On further investigation, I
found a much later ad in the
July 1941 *Bulletin of the New
York Academy of Medicine.* By
then, Mr. Arthur C. Pomeroy
had offices in Newark, Boston,
Springfield, Detroit and
Wilkes-Barre[208] and had had
many locations in Brooklyn,
the Bronx and Manhattan. By
1941, the Pomeroy "empire"
heralded:

*The Pomeroy Frame Truss
embodies the knowledge and
experience of seventy years.
Its time-proven effectiveness
in retaining herniae through
passive resistance, rather
than through active pressure,
has won the recognition and
approbation of countless
physicians through three
generations.*

*There is no guarantee
of truss satisfaction greater
than the combination of
POMEROY skill and
experience as exemplified in
the POMEROY FRAME
TRUSS.*[209]

My search to connect
the disparate pieces of
information on the Internet
ended with a pleasant
surprise. Beth Beeman, the
great-great-granddaughter
of Mr. Pomeroy, confirmed
that the grave site in
Green-Wood Cemetery
in Brooklyn,[210] with the
birth and death dates of
December 12, 1873, and
December 30, 1956, belongs
to the same man who helped
sustain a prosthetic limb and

abdominal belt empire in the
state with the same moniker.
Beeman also confirmed that
his father, Daniel Pomeroy,
founded the business in
1867 and passed it along
to his son, who graduated
from Wesleyan University
with a bachelor's degree in
philosophy in 1895.

In our e-mail exchanges,
it was also confirmed that
the May 3, 1903 *New York
Times* obituary for three-
year-old Ruth Elizabeth
Pomeroy,[211] daughter of
Arthur Cleveland Pomeroy
who died of scarlet fever, was
indeed the oldest sister of
Beeman's grandmother and
for whom Beeman's mother, a
published poet,[212] was named.
At eighty-three years of age,
Mr. Pomeroy experienced
the loss of a young child,
completed a valued education
in a prestigious university,
inherited a thriving business
and lived way past the
expected lifespan of an
American male in his time.
This sign is a testament to
Pomeroy's legacy.

Assorted Signs on 32ND

(pages 200–201)

G. Schoepfer Glass Eyes & Taxidermist Supplies

Cottage Restaurant—Home Cooked Food

Fotoshop—Motion Picture Equipment—Same Day Service.

According to Grutchfield, Gustav Schoepfer (1891–1988) first opened his business on East 95th Street in Brooklyn about 1917 and "manufactured, exported and imported glass eyes and other items for toy makers, opticians and taxidermists." In his research, Grutchfield was surprised to discover the eyes were used by milliners and for dolls and stuffed toys. Beaks were manufactured for taxidermists. In 1921, Schoepfer opened his first Manhattan location at 106 East 12th Street and relocated to several sites in the West 30s area during the late 1920s before settling at 132 West 32nd Street from 1931 until 1939. This sign was at that location, dating from the 1930s. Grutchfield asserts that as of June 2003, "G. Schoepfer, Inc. still exists (in Cheshire, Conn.) as a major supplier of glass and acrylic eyes; optical goods and optometrists equipment and supplies."

Grutchfield goes on to say that the first Cottage Restaurant was referred to as a tearoom and was located on Lexington Avenue near Bloomingdale's on East 58th Street from about 1924. The restaurant's president, George H. Rice, was born in Mississippi, and his wife, Miriam (secretary and treasurer), hailed from Louisiana. The 1930 U.S. Census listed their ages as twenty-nine and twenty-eight, respectively. The Cottage Restaurant opened at 132 West 32nd Street in 1926 and remained open until the early 1970s.[213]

The sign below and to the right says "Fotoshop, Cameras, Motion Picture Equipment, Photo Finishing, Same Day Service." It's ironic that decades after this sign was painted and the store it advertised closed, I am using a computer program called Photoshop to decipher its contents.

Wm. W. Pecan Undertaker & Embalmer

1666 B'way. 2nd Door Above Meat Market

Is it just me, or does this sound like the plot for a Stephen Sondheim musical? According to Brooklyn Genealogy Information dot com, W.W. Pecan started his undertaker establishment at 570 Grand Street in the Eastern Division. Pecan's livery stables were located at 279 Graham Avenue near Grand Street. In addition to his service to

Wm. W. Pecan Undertaker & Embalmer—under the Broadway el in Bushwick, Brooklyn. Taken March 1999. Sign circa late 1890s.

the community as undertaker and embalmer, he also served for five years as the assistant foreman of the Volunteer Hook & Ladder Co., No. 2.[214] Pecan's business listing and short bio were transcribed for this website:

Furnishing Undertaker, Livery and Boarding Stables, Coffin Wareroom
…Among those following the undertaking business in Brooklyn no one is better known or more universally esteemed than Mr. Wm. W. Pecan. This gentleman established his business here in 1859, and has been located at his present address since 1862. At this point he occupies a fine office and wareroom, and carries a complete assortment of coffins, caskets, and general funeral furnishing requisites. He does an extensive business as a funeral director and embalmer, and his services are in frequent demand.

In addition to his undertaking business Mr. Pecan carries on a large livery and boarding stable business. His stables… are thoroughly equipped throughout. He runs two coaches, five light wagons, and ten fine horses, and

also has accommodations for boarding twelve horses. Mr. Pecan is a native of New York City.[215]

The building where Wm. W. Pecan's original office was located, on the corner of Lorimer and Grand Streets, is still standing. However, Pecan's Graham Avenue stables have since been demolished, and a new building is in their place. This particular building pictured in the sign was located farther south and east on the south side of Broadway, even farther toward the eastern border of Brooklyn and Queens, closer to Trinity Cemetery and Cemetery of the Evergreens. This building has since been remodeled and stuccoed and has had a new building built adjacently to it, obscuring any evidence that this was once a thriving funeral parlor—*and* meat market.

As you drive along the scenic Jackie Robinson Parkway (formerly the Interborough), with the best skyline Manhattan views, you are surrounded by the hundreds of thousands of graves of the likes of the Dutch modernist painter Pieter Cornelis Mondriaan of Amersfoort; jazz musician and composer Eubie Blake;

and the countless known and lesser-known veterans from the Revolutionary and Civil Wars to the major wars and conflicts of the twentieth century. James T. "Pop" Young (Young & Schmuck) is buried at the Evergreens, as well as jazz tenor sax player Lester Young and dancer Bill "Bojangles" Robinson of the song "Mr. Bojangles"[216] and the eight women listed as unknown from the Triangle Shirtwaist Fire of 1911.[217] And who knows of the countless bodies that were interred by Mr. Wm. W. Pecan, Undertaker & Embalmer of the Eastern Division of Brooklyn, during his long and esteemed tenure. The countless stories of the people who struggled, conquered, lost and died still linger on the sides of brick faces throughout New York City's five boroughs in fading ads. One day, just take a brisk or leisurely stroll with your head up and perhaps you will see this magnificent and ever-changing city through these eyes. At the risk of being nostalgic, I'd say do it for old times' sake.

Fading Ads and a Transatlantic Relationship

I have never met Frank Jump, but he has, perhaps unknowingly, been a major influence on my life over the last five years. It all started for me in Stoke Newington, an area of North London in the UK where I grew up. In early 2006, I looked up and saw something I had never noticed before. "Fount Pens Repaired," it said, a sign painted on the first and second floors of the building in front of me. Farther down the street, I spotted another, this time promoting "Alf, the Purse King." At the time I just walked on, unaware of how important this writing on the walls would become to me.

In the summer that year, I mentioned these pieces of hand-painted advertising to my girlfriend (now wife), saying that I thought they should be photographed before they disappeared. She encouraged me to "just get on with it," words she would later come to (partially) regret. I set about taking pictures and sending these to friends to ask if they knew of further locations. I also tried to research their history. Two things happened at this point: first was an overwhelmingly positive reaction from the people I had e-mailed; second was discovering Frank Jump's Fading Ad site.

Frank's site and my communications with him encouraged me to pursue this new interest further. I was surprised how little information existed online about what Frank refers to as "fading ads." His diligent work documenting signs in the United States, and across the world, gave me the idea to do something similar for signs in my own country. Frank is more than just an enthusiast; he is a passionate educator, and I learned a lot from him as I considered what to do next.

Things soon started to move quickly. I was inundated with locations and photos from friends and family and soon had a sizable collection of material. Again inspired by Frank, I set up my first blog called *Brickads*, a name I gave to what I would later refer to as *Ghostsigns*. The blog allowed me to publish the material I was gathering. Press and public interest followed. This led to me forging a link with the History of Advertising Trust and starting a project to create a permanent online archive of hand-painted advertising in the UK and Ireland. From announcing the project to launching the archive took exactly one year. It now includes over seven hundred images, each recording a piece of advertising and social history for future generations. It takes them back to a time when people had their fountain pens repaired and Alf was the self-proclaimed "Purse King."

Like Frank, I have dedicated a significant part of my life to photographing and researching these fading ads. In doing so, Frank finds meaning at a very personal level, providing a metaphor through which to explore his own survival against the odds with HIV/AIDS. For me, I think it started with a belief that something should be done to document these historical artifacts and then a passion developing in response to people's reactions to the idea. In the absence of anyone else taking on the task, I felt an obligation to do so.

Both Frank and I personify the signs in our writing, suggesting an emotional connection with our subjects. Perhaps this is what stimulates me to care, working to save their memory before they pass away from natural or man-made causes. I am not a supporter of legal protection measures, as the signs have managed for long enough without them. However, through photography, Frank and others like him can extend their sell-by date indefinitely.

Sam Roberts
UK Brickads
www.ghostsigns.co.uk

The Collaged City

Painted wall signs in cities beckoned nineteenth-century Americans to soothe their nerves with Omega Oil, brighten their clothes with Reckitt's Blueing, snack on Uneeda Biscuits and restore their energy with Coca-Cola. The rise of national brands and consumer culture made commercial images dance in bright colors at a giant scale up and down city walls. Some thought it was part of the reckless energy of the new world and a byproduct of the hectic press of American business. But others drew back in disgust, decrying the visual nuisance that seized the public's eye for constant huckstering. This clash between commerce and culture found a powerful expression in the City Beautiful movement of the early twentieth century that sought to reform cities aesthetically, as well as morally. The City Beautiful improvement program included creating sculpture competitions, fine municipal buildings, parks and wide boulevards but also targeted signs and billboards that would compete with its program of civic pride and uplift. At the very same time, national advertisers were organizing coast-to-coast campaigns and the outdoor advertising industry was consolidating its political power in a trade association to advance its interests and defend itself from City Beautiful–inspired regulations.

Wrigley's Spearmint Gum created giant electric signs in Times Square, painted walls and bought space in the streetcars that whizzed city dwellers from home to work. Not only did the habit of chewing gum alarm the upper crust, but they also feared that the sight of large, luscious lips on gum ads might topple the moral order. The National Biscuit Company, with its pioneering packaged crackers, lavished $7 million on advertising in the first decade of the twentieth century. Its iconic kid in the yellow slicker aimed to remind readers that these wrapped national brand crackers were sealed against moisture. The accompanying jingle, "lest you forget, we say it yet, Uneeda biscuit," played a similar memory strategy with words: blithely coining a name and spelling for the cracker that made teachers cringe. The ubiquitous advertisements charmed enough of the public to ensure a healthy corporate future for Nabisco, but they also provided visual and grammatical fuel to the firestorm of cultural criticism of outdoor advertising. Another famous example of visual vinegar was the giant lighted Heinz pickle on the Hotel Cumberland at Madison Square,

Uneeda Biscuit—Fifteenth Street and Fourth Avenue, Park Slope, Brooklyn. Taken August 2003.

which gave off an orange glow in 1899. What especially annoyed critics in this case was how the electric sign outshone the nearby Dewy Arch, a typical City Beautiful piece of civic uplift celebrating the victory in the Spanish-American War in Cuba and the Philippines. The juxtaposition of civic art and advertisement was common: advertisers, of course, sought the most prominent placements in areas with high visibility. For example, Christopher Columbus, presiding over his circle at 59th Street, overlooked in 1913 a giant sign for Kelly tires with a cute gal smiling from within the rim, and on a taller building behind it, an enormous rubric proclaimed "Gainsborough Studios."

These examples illustrate the clash between sign haters and advertisers at a time when the American public was beginning to develop a range of responses to ads. Initially, the public often seemed delighted by the signs: they were novel, a form of free entertainment, one of the amusing sights to eyeball in cities. But as national brands and national advertising campaigns became more and more assertive, a growing opposition movement turned to politics and government to fight the ads.

Just before World War I, reformers of New York's Municipal Art Society had proposed a Billboard Commission to regulate signs, hoping to decrease their size, control their placement and tone down the "glaring colors" that so offended the city's aesthetic police. Commission members spoke of their duty to protect "the public's sense of sight" and charged that "disgusting billboard advertisments…rob the people of their rightful heritage of natural beauty." O.J. Gude, who was head of one of the biggest outdoor advertising companies in New York, was clever enough to have joined a committee of the Municipal Art Society, which was pushing for reform. He commented that

tourists were coming to Times Square to see the electric signs, which had admirers even in France, and implied that "beauty" was in the eyes of the beholder rather than a legislative concept. Gude's compatriots in the business had been practicing the art of populism for some years already in their trade journal, *The Billposter*. "But it is simply ridiculous to howl about the nuisance of billboards in those locations where the monotonous dullness and deadness of the view is enough to give one the blues…far from debasing the tastes of passersby, they are refreshing as signs of life amid the brick and stone Saharas of the great city," wrote one advertiser in 1903.

Heinz Factory—Bergen Street and Franklin Avenue, Prospect Heights, Brooklyn. Taken July 1999.

O.J. Gude Company of NY—Select Brand—Grade A Milk—Coney Island Avenue, Flatbush, Brooklyn. Taken August 1999.

advertisers were understanding something important about evolving habits of perception. Walter Dill Scott, a professor of psychology at Northwestern University, studied Omega Oil advertisements in the early twentieth century. He wrote in his influential 1902 *Theory of Advertising*: "Omega Oil is not only a thing which can be applied and felt by the skin, but it is also a thing that can be seen and smelt." Scott emphasized that the Omega headline "It's Green," which appeared meaningless, actually sparked a pleasant association and mood and concluded that Omega Oil ads succeeded by appealing to the senses, which evoked strong mental images in the consumer. Dill's analysis of the emotive power of advertising seemed novel and startling at the time and draws our attention to the seductive power of the imagery, rather than the notion of coercive selling that made reformers so indignant.

Indeed, it is that seductive power that has persisted long after the advertising messages have lost their meaning. And the seduction derives from the urban contexts of billboards, light displays and wall signs—the dynamics of viewers and signs—as much as from the individual compositions. In cities that are constantly being torn down and rebuilt, old things can become the object of considerable nostalgic affection, quite apart from their overt content, such as cigarette advertising or long-ago patent medicine pitches. Where once a patent medicine make suggested "children cry for Castoria," his sweet laxative syrup, nowadays the ad itself is the syrup. Furthermore, I would suggest that the gigantic scale of the wall signs gives them a kind of supernatural power at an unconscious level, as though the line were spoken by something larger than life, a force

Maybe reformers who argued against painted wall signs using the cultural terms generated by the conventions of painting were missing the cultural dynamics behind the impact of commercial imagery. As advertising began to use testing and research, the gap between the language City Beautiful reformers used to describe the experience of the urban dwellers and the actual experience of those seeing these large advertisements demonstrated that bigger than an individual such as the state, a society or even subliminally—the gods. Cultural critic Susan Stewart discusses the gigantic as something experienced in relation to the scale of the human body, and thus the gigantic becomes "a metaphor for the abstract authority of the state and the collective, public life." These psychological dimensions of the scale, color and familiarity of advertising in urban contexts move us from the literal meanings of signs to a consideration of how they appear in a welter of tall buildings, crisscross patterns of light and vistas framed by the canyons of avenues and belts of illuminated elevated trains.

City observers perceive signs as part of a collage of sensations rather than as individual and discrete messages and objects. Imagine the city observer as a stroller—what the nineteenth-century Parisians celebrated as a *flaneur*—who watches the ever-changing spectacle of scurrying people against an unplanned scenography of building angles, sign fragments, windows silhouetted like movie stills and flash frames created by traffic lights. This is the visual and psychological collage that gives the old wall signs their persistent significance in the city. Thus, when we isolate rare and now precious images of wall signs, we may lose sight of the fundamental texture of how people experience them in the city. Fortunately, Frank Jump's astute framing of the remains of wall signs around New York City often has clues to those contexts. For example, "Philip Morris, America's Finest Cigarette" includes a rich deep background with the World Trade Center towers glimpsed in the distance down the avenue. This framing implies a kind of looking that a period passerby might well have done: catching a cigarette pitch from the side of the eye, while keeping an eye for

action on the street and scanning the horizon for clouds massing off the harbor behind the towers at the tip of Manhattan. In other cases, Jump wittily reminds us that the signs and the buildings are transient objects, apt to be draped with ivy, or scorched by the sun, or obscured by the cheeky spray of graffiti writers. Or he simply lets us savor the irony of the juxtaposed "Cottage Restaurant's home cooked food" next to the "taxidermist's supplies." And for modern-day gals who never pressed a sewing machine treadle to the ground, "Seely Shoulder shapes" is a tongue twister, not a dressmaker's notion.

The phrases and shapes jumbled into an urban vocabulary of looking have become part of the rhetoric of the city, a part of the urban texture we expect in places built before the car, when brick was red and paint was so full of lead it lasted for generations (while making the billposters tremble with the side effects of lead poisoning over a lifetime). As people have learned to appreciate cities as layered accumulations of civic infrastructure, built environment, vernacular expression, commercial culture, populist marking and yes, even formal architecture, the place of the faded wall sign has assumed a role as an essential part of the fabric. According to urban historian Kevin Lynch, old signs can help make the city legible and may form part of the saturated memories that give a city meaning and function as landmarks, helping people to orient themselves. In a built environment as rapidly changing as New York, the persistence of old signs that peek from behind sleek new skyscrapers can offer a reassuring sense of continuity. Old signs have become part of a new rhetoric of urban preservation in which not just architecture but the visual look of neighborhoods becomes the objects of historic marking. It is fascinating to realize that in New York, the Municipal Art Society, which in the Progressive era fought the sign, became attuned to the role of signs as part of a common visual heritage and helped write rules to *require* them in the redeveloped Times Square area in the 1980s.

In the course of more than 150 years of walls signs painted tall upon city brick, urban dwellers have come to like them. From targets of ire, derided as visual junk and architectural desecration, wall signs have become objects of appreciation and preservation. And in the process of learning to look and learning to like them, the public has shaped notions of common visual rights. Spotting old signs and interpreting them as interesting pieces of the urban fabric has become a populist history sport—something that would have astounded a City Beautiful advocate and yet might, somehow, please him in the long run, as he saw his goal of city appreciation being ultimately fulfilled.

Kathleen Hulser, public historian
New-York Historical Society
July 2011

Notes

On Advertising Legend Douglas Leigh

1. American Sign Museum, www.signmuseum.net.

New York City's Fading Ad Campaign

2. Read: Frank H. Jump, Interview #33, ACT-UP Oral History Project, Sarah Schulman, www.actuporalhistory.org/interviews/images/jump.pdf; or watch video excerpt, *Are You on the List?* www.actuporalhistory.org/interviews/interviews_06.html#jump.
3. The Estate Project: for artists with AIDS, Alliance for the Arts, www.artistswithaids.org.
4. Fading Ads: The Photography of Frank H. Jump, *Archaeology Online* (October 20, 1998), www.archaeology.org/online/features/ads.
5. Stephen Greco, "Signs of Life: Photographer Frank Jump Captures Traces of a Lost World, *POZ Magazine* (November 1998), www.poz.com/articles/233_1666.shtml.
6. Web Guide: Hot Sites, Fading Ads, *USA Today* (updated April 2003), www.usatoday.com/tech/webguide/hotsites/2002-09-11-hotsites.htm.
7. Missy Sullivan, "Artist Power," *Forbes Magazine* (May 22, 2000), www.forbes.com/forbes/2000/0522/036.html.
8. *London Observer Magazine*, "Signs of the Times," (May 3, 1999), www.frankjump.com/londonobserver.pdf.
9. BIT, "Brooklyn Review: The Fading Ad Blog, Best of Brooklyn Independent Television," December 29, 2010, www.fadingad.com/fadingadblog/?p=7639.
10. Kevin Walsh, *Forgotten New York*, www.forgotten-ny.com.
11. Walter Grutchfield, *New York City Signs: 14th to 42nd Street*, www.14to42.net.
12. Sam Roberts, *Ghostsigns Blog*, www.ghostsigns.co.uk/blog.
13. Joseph Berger, "Fading Memories," *New York Times*, November 5, 2005, query.nytimes.com/gst/fullpage.html?res=9B07E6DF143EF936A35752C1A9639C8B63.
14. Gregory and Maria Pearce, "Pasolini: Quo Vadis? The Fate of Pier Paolo Pasolini," www.cinemaseekers.com/Pasolinitext.html.
15. Nostalgia: Fading Ad Wiki, fadingad.wikispaces.com/Nostalgia.
16. PBS, "Channel Thirteen's Life Part Two, with Professor Gerald Torres of The University of Texas (Austin)," www.pbs.org/lifepart2/watch/season-1/adapting-change/adapting-change-transcript.
17. *Fading Ad Blog*, "Penmanship Stupid—Faux Ad—Jerry "Orange" Johnson, www.fadingad.com/fadingadblog/?p=8732.
18. *Agility Nut*, "Super Signage: Penmanship Sign (gone)," www.agilitynut.com/signs/nyc.html.
19. Leila Abboud, "The Wall Dogs' Last Stand: Technology Puts Sign Painters Out of Work," Columbia School of Journalism Website, www.jrn.columbia.edu/studentwork/cns/2002-03-20/244.asp (dead link).

Snake Oils, Elixirs, Tonics, Cure-alls and Laxatives

20. Wikipedia, "Snake oil," en.wikipedia.org/wiki/Snake_oil.
21. Online Etymology Dictionary, "Elixir," www.etymonline.com/index.php?term=elixir.
22. U.S. Department of Health and Human Services, U.S. Food and Drug Administration History, www.fda.gov/AboutFDA/WhatWeDo/History/default.htm.
23. Up To Date, "lipodystrophic syndromes," www.uptodate.com/contents/lipodystrophic-syndromes?source=search_result&selectedTitle=1~2.

24. Kelly Pilson, MEd, *Your Health Online Magazine*, "Chemotherapy, Ototoxicity & the Inner Ear," September 20, 2007, www.yourhealthmagazine.net/articles/cancer-awareness/1064-Chemotherapy,-Ototoxicity-.html?-the-Inner-Ear=.

25. Caroline Rance, The Quack Doctor, "Omega Oil," March 10, 2010, thequackdoctor.com/index.php/the-omega-oil.

26. Julian Seery Gude, "O.J. Gude and Me," *Julians.name*, December 18, 2005, www.blog.julians.name/2005/12/18/oj-gude-and-me.

27. Sandra Walker, RI, sandrawalkerri.com/about_sandra.htm.

28. Fading Ad Campaign, "Sandra Walker," www.frankjump.com/sandrawalker.html (*Omega Oil*, watercolour, 2003).

29. *Urban Dictionary*, "alter kaker," www.urbandictionary.com/define.php?term=altercocker.

30. *The 20th Century Song Book*, Chattanooga Medicine Company, 1904, www.mum.org/songbk1.htm.

31. Wiktionary, "Syrup of figs," en.wiktionary.org/wiki/syrup_of_figs.

32. D. Sikrov, MD, "Hemorrhoids Are the Consequence of the Sitting Defecation Posture," www.sikiron.com/pages/150_bowl.php.

33. PubMed, "Health benefits of dietary fiber," U.S. National Library of Medicine National Institutes of Health, www.ncbi.nlm.nih.gov/pubmed/19335713.

34. Let's Move, "America's Move to Raise a Healthier Generation of Kids," Childhood Obesity Task Force Report, www.letsmove.gov/about.

35. The Centaur Company, www.centaur.com (established 1871).

36. *New York Times*, "A free gift; To the American people. What the Federal troops are fighting to sustain," October 23, 1861 (archive), www.nytimes.com/1861/10/23/news/free-gift-american-people-what-federal-troops-are-fighting-sustain-our-soldiers.html?pagewanted=2.

37. *New York Times*, "A new method of curing certain diseases by the use of Radway's Ready Relief," December 4, 1863 (archive), www.nytimes.com/1863/12/04/news/a-new-method-of-curing-certain-diseases-by-the-use-of-radway-s-ready-relief.html.

38. John Knowles Paine, "Radway's Ready Relief," Music Library of the Harvard College Library, January 31, 1960, books.google.com/books?id=HGERAAAAYAAJ&pg=PP11#v=onepage&q&f=false.

39. Walsh, "I'm still standing, RKO Bushwick," *Forgotten NY*, www.forgotten-ny.com/STREET%20SCENES/RKO%20Bushwick/RKO.html.

40. Robert Pozarycki, "Elmhurst Park Grows: Working to Replace Tanks with Greenspace," *Times Newsweekly Online*, August 19, 2010, www.timesnewsweekly.com/news/2010-08-19/Local_News/ELMHURST_____PK_GROWS.html.

41. See Blustein ad: www.14to42.net/images/blustein-1920.jpg.

42. Grutchfield, *New York City Signs: 14th to 42nd Street*, www.14to42.net/27street3.5.html.

43. Michael Gallagher, "Ginseng, John Jacob Astor, and the Chinese trade," *JSTOR Plant Science*, February 25, 2011, jstorplants.org/2011/02/25/ginseng-john-jacob-astor-and-the-chinese-trade.

44. Dr. David Wang, "Ginseng: The herb that helped U.S. commerce," *World Huaren Federation*, www.huaren.org/Text/1204731076687-9411/pC/1204726261750-6644.

45. Sidecar Brooklyn, www.sidecarbrooklyn.com/wall.html.

DAYS WITH ART

46. "Dr. Tucker's 59 for all pain, Confrontation," Fading Ad Campaign, frankjump.com/045.html.

FOOD, SNACKS AND CANDY

47. George Taylor, *Martyrs to the Revolution in the British Prison-ships in the Wallabout Bay* (New York: W.H. Arthur & Company Stationers, 1855) books.google.com/books?id=dR1CAAAAIAAJ&dq=Wallabout&pg=PA24#v=onepage&q&f=false.

48. Nicole Brydson, "Navy Yard dive not dead yet, building for sale," *Brooklyn The Borough*, February 2009, www.brooklyntheborough.com/2009/02/navy-yard-dive-not-dead-yet.

49. Better Living New Zealand, "What are other kinds of ham," www.betterliving.co.nz/content/athome/cooking/what-are-other-kinds-of-ham.aspx.

50. Urban Dictionary, "gabagool," www.urbandictionary.com/define.php?term=gabagool.

51. Richard Cohen, *Sweet and Low: A Family Story* (New York: Farrar, Straus, Giroux, 2006) www.npr.org/templates/story/story.php?storyId=5418961.

52. Wikipedia, "Sodium cyclamate," en.wikipedia.org/wiki/Sodium_cyclamate.

53. Charles E. Ophardt, Virtual Chembook, "cyclamate," Elmhurst College, Illinois (2003), www.elmhurst.edu/~chm/vchembook/549cyclamate.html.

54. Cohen, *Sweet and Low*.

55. *Daily Beast* (*Newsweek*), "Five controversial food additives," www.newsweek.com/2008/03/12/five-controversial-food-additives.html.

56. "An FDA guide to sweeteners on the market," NPR Books, www.npr.org/templates/story/story.php?storyId=5418961.

57. United States Environmental Protection Agency, "EPA Removes Saccharin from Hazardous Substances Listing," yosemite.epa.gov/opa/admpress.nsf/d0cf6618525a9efb85257359003fb69d/ea895a11ea50a56d852577f9005e2690!OpenDocument.

58. New Fulton Fish Market Cooperative at Hunts Point, Inc., "History," www.newfultonfishmarket.com/history.html.

59. The City of New York Business Integrity Commission, www.nyc.gov/html/bic/html/home/home.shtml.

60. Frederick R. Black, "Jamaica Bay: A History," Gateway National Recreation Area New York, New Jersey–Washington, D.C., 1981, www.nps.gov/history/history/online_books/gate/jamaica_bay_hrs.pdf.

61. Report of the Commissioner of Agriculture for the Year 1879 (Washington, D.C.: Government Printing Office, 1880), books.google.com/books?id=XGgTAAAAYAAJ&pg=PA438&sig=oyaxBA84xc5AYVb00nH02Gq8iQw&hl=en#v=onepage&q&f=false].

62. Walsh, "Dairies," Forgotten New York, www.forgotten-ny.com/SIGNS/dairies/dairies.html.

63. Rabbi Jeffrey A. Marx, "Historical Outline of Breakstone Brothers Dairy," Breghshtein Family Website, December 2007, www.breakstone.us/Dairyhistory.htm#_edn37.

64. Fading Ad Blog, "W.M. Evans Dairy Co. Inc.—3480 Fulton Street—Cypress Hills, Brooklyn," March 26, 2008, www.fadingad.com/fadingadblog/?p=1120.

65. Wikipedia, "Baby Ruth," en.wikipedia.org/wiki/Baby_Ruth.

66. Fading Ad Campaign, "Planter Peanuts Repro Collage," March 1999, frankjump.com/037.html.

67. Walsh, "Forgotten Ads of Queens," Forgotten New York, www.forgotten-ny.com/ADS/Ads%20in%20Queens/queens.html.

68. Fading Ad Blog, "Missing Mr. Peanut in Wilkes-Barre, PA," November 30, 2008, www.fadingad.com/fadingadblog/?p=2572.

69. Denise Allabaugh, "Former Planters Building on South Main Street Being Razed for Strip Mall," Citizen's Voice, August 15, 2006, www.myspace.com/nepa_ypa/blog/287250044.

70. Advertising Age, "Advertising history timeline," 2005, adage.com/century/timeline.

71. Gold Medal Flour, "Our Heritage," www.gmflour.com/gmflour/ourheritage.aspx.

72. Chicago Advertising Federation, "Greatest Ads," www.chicagoadfed.org/i4a/pages/index.cfm?pageid=3281.

73. For more Gold Medal Flour ads: www.frankjump.com/goldmedal.html.

74. Sojourner Farms, "The History of Pet Food," www.sojos.com/historyofpetfood.html.

75. Pet Food Institute, "Pet Food History," www.petfoodinstitute.org/petfoodhistory.htm.

76. Fading Ad Blog, Cadet Dog Food—Maspeth, Queens—Richard Boll," June 29, 2009, www.fadingad.com/fadingadblog/?p=4167.

A Coke and a Smoke

77. Wikipedia, "pentimento," en.wikipedia.org/wiki/Pentimento.

78. Logo Blog, "Coca-Cola logo," www.logoblog.org/coca_cola_logo.php.

79. James A. Shaw, "'Perfect Satisfaction' from Arabia 1912–1915," Jim's Burnt Offerings, www.jimsburntofferings.com/packsmecca.html.

80. Walsh, Forgotten New York, www.forgotten-ny.com/ADS/newgaryads/ads.html.

81. "The Disadvantages of You," the Brass Ring, Dunhill Records (1967), youtu.be/0lr_s4bGnoA.

82. Smoker's History, "Philip Morris's Predecessor, Benson & Hedges," last modified on June 13, 2011, www.smokershistory.com/Benson.html.

83. Wikipedia, "Altria," en.wikipedia.org/wiki/Altria.

84. Randy James, "Cigarette Advertising," Time magazine, June 15, 2009, www.time.com/time/magazine/article/0,9171,1905530,00.html#ixzz1SHmZhuK2.

85. Ibid.

86. Information Research Lab, "Smoking Deaths Worldwide," www.inforesearchlab.com/smokingdeaths.chtml.

87. Mickey Stretton, et al., "Chronometry," New Masters of Flash Annual, www.frankjump.com/mastersflash1.pdf.

Breweriana

88. Advertising Beer Tray, "Liberty Beer—Tamo' Shanter Ale 'American Brewing Co., Rochester, N.Y.'" trayman.net/TrayDetail/Script/Liberty%20Beer.htm.

89. Fading Ad Blog, "Knopf Clothier as Seen from High Falls Mills—Genesee River—Rochester, NY," August 8, 2010, www.fadingad.com/fadingadblog/?p=6935.

90. Ruth Rosenberg-Naperstack, "A Brief History of Brewing in Rochester," Rochester History 54, no. 2 (Spring 1992): 9, www.rochester.lib.ny.us/~rochhist/v54_1992/v54i2.pdf.

91. Ibid., 3–4.

92. Ibid., 16.

93. Ibid., 4.

94. Wikipedia, "Rochester, New York," en.wikipedia.org/wiki/Rochester,_New_York.

95. fadingad.wordpress.com/2007/06/24/sam-roberts-uk-ghost-ads-on-colossal-media.

96. Jess Kidden, "Guinness in America," sites.google.com/site/jesskidden/guinnessinamerica.

City of Immigrants and the Mack Sign Company

97. Grutchfield, *New York City Signs: 14th to 42nd Street,* "Mack Brothers Sign Co.," www.14to42.net/mack.html.

Shoes, Hats and Assorted Garments—Wholesale and Retail

98. Grutchfield, *New York City Signs: 14th to 42nd Street,* "United Thread Mills," www.14to42.net/unitedthread.htm.
99. *Fading Ad Blog,* "United Thread Mills in Transition—East Houston Street, NYC 1998," March 6, 2008, www.fadingad.com/fadingadblog/?p=1042.
100. Dana Rubin and Otto Luna, "Seely Shoulder Shapes," Manhattan Ghost Signs Digital Collection, ghostsignsnyc.omeka.net/items/show/47.
101. Artkraft Strauss, "Senior Management," www.artkraft.com/staff.html.
102. Tama Starr and Edward Heyman, *Signs & Wonders* (New York: Doubleday, 1998), 19–21.
103. New York Public Library Digital Collection, "Manhattan: Union Square (East)," digitalgallery.nypl.org/nypldigital/dgkeysearchdetail.cfm?strucID=413425&imageID=723622F.
104. Grutchfield, *New York City Signs: 14th to 42nd Street,* "Crown Coat Front Company," www.14to42.net/16street.html.
105. NYPL Digital Library, digitalgallery.nypl.org/nypldigital/dgkeysearchdetail.cfm?strucID=413425&imageID=723622F.
106. "New York Notes," *The Jewelers Circular* 85, no. 2, January 17, 1923, books.google.com/books?id=4EEcAQAAMAAJ&lpg=RA7-PA99&ots=GC0bdtAxOH&dq=Mogi%2C%20Momomoi%20%26%20Company%2C&pg=RA7-PA99#v=onepage&q=Mogi,%20Momomoi%20&%20Company,&f=false.
107. Wikipedia, "aleph," en.wikipedia.org/wiki/Aleph.
108. Libby Tucker, "Cropsey at Camp," New York Folklore Society, *Voices* 32 (Fall–Winter 2006), www.nyfolklore.org/pubs/voic32-3-4/gspirits.html.
109. Wikipedia, "Golem," en.wikipedia.org/wiki/Golem.
110. Dan Bilefsky, "Hard Times Give New Life to Prague's Golem," *New York Times,* May 10, 2009, www.nytimes.com/2009/05/11/world/europe/11golem.html.
111. Grutchfield, *New York City Signs: 14th to 42nd Street,* "Weber & Heilbroner ad," www.14to42.net/images/weber&heilbroner1904.jpg.
112. Grutchfield, *New York City Signs: 14th to 42nd Street,* "Weber & Heilbroner," www.14to42.net/34streetw047.html.
113. Mary Bellis, "History of the Elevator," inventors.about.com/library/inventors/blelevator.htm.
114. Grutchfield, *New York City Signs: 14th to 42nd Street,* "Miss Weber Millinery," www.14to42.net/22street2.html.
115. University of Wisconsin Digital Collection, "All Sewn Up: Millinery, Dressmaking, Clothing and Costume," digital.library.wisc.edu/1711.dl/HumanEcol.MillineryBooks.
116. Wikipedia, "Mad as a hatter," en.wikipedia.org/wiki/Mad_as_a_hatter.
117. Funding Universe, "R.H. Macy & Co., Company History," www.fundinguniverse.com/company-histories/R-H-Macy-amp;-Co-Inc-Company-History.html.
118. Jason Maoz, "Retail Kings," *Jewish Press,* January 25, 2006, www.jewishpress.com/printArticle.cfm?contentid=18350.
119. Straus Historical Society, "Lazarus and Sara Straus Family," www.straushistoricalsociety.org/l_ss.php.
120. Fund Universe, www.fundinguniverse.com/company-histories/R-H-Macy-amp;-Co-Inc-Company-History.html.
121. Walsh, *Forgotten New York,* "Walking on Graham Avenue," www.forgotten-ny.com/STREET SCENES/manhattan.graham/graham.html.
122. *Brooklyn Daily Eagle,* "Berger-Aufrecht," October 20, 1929, B5 fultonhistory.com/Newspaper%205/Brooklyn%20NY%20Daily%20Eagle/Brooklyn%20NY%20Daily%20Eagle%201929%20Grayscale/Brooklyn%20NY%20Daily%20Eagle%201929%20a%20Grayscale%20-%201219.pdf.
123. Ibid.

Might as Well jUmP!

124. Walsh, *Forgotten New York,* www.forgotten-ny.com/STREET SCENES/RKO Bushwick/RKO.html.
125. Fading Ad Campaign, "RKO Bushwick," www.fadingad.com/bushwick.html.
126. Walsh, Forgotten New York, www.forgotten-ny.com/forgottoners/coney3.html.
127. Fading Ad Campaign, www.fadingad.com/dailynews.html.
128. Fading Ad Campaign, www.fadingad.com/rosariodawson.html.
129. Walsh, Forgotten New York, www.forgotten-ny.com/SLICES/jump/jump.html.

Laundry Products, Washing Machines and Real Estate

130. David W. Dunlap, "Old York; Look Close, and in This Ever-New Town You Will See Traces of the Past Peeking Through," *New York Times,* December 12, 2000, section 14, page 1, column 5, www.nytimes.com/2000/12/10/nyregion/old-york-look-close-this-ever-new-town-you-will-see-traces-past-peeking-through.html.

131. Bendix, "Bendix Spirit of Invention," www.bendixappliances.com/about.
132. "Bendix Home Appliances, Inc.," patent search, Espace, worldwide.espacenet.com/publicationDetails/biblio?CC=US&NR=2165884&KC=&FT=E&locale=en_EP.
133. Fading Ad Campaign, "Bendix Home Laundry," www.frankjump.com/031.html.
134. *New York Times*, "Emil Talamini," obituary, October 29, 1970, query.nytimes.com/mem/archive/pdf?res=F70B17FD3C5F1B7493CBAB178BD95F448785F9.

JEWELRY AND ACCESSORIES

135. Grutchfield, *New York City Signs: 14th to 42nd Street*, "Shield's Jewelry," www.14to42.net/31street1.5.html.
136. New York First, www.newyorkfirst.com/gifts/7064.html.
137. Andrew Britton, *Katherine Hepburn: Star as Feminist* (New York: Columbia University Press: 1984), 238, books.google.com/books?id=PP4S2-VBXYoC&lpg=PA238&ots=wT9hpXCEdA&dq=Katherine%20Hepburn%20the%20Flatiron&pg=PA238#v=onepage&q&f=false.
138. Wikipedia, "bobby pin," en.wikipedia.org/wiki/Bobby_pin.
139. Grutchfield, *New York City Signs: 14th to 42nd Street*, "The Griffon Cutlery Works," www.14to42.net/19street3.html.
140. Randy Kennedy, "Saving Images of 'Dead Signs' on Old Walls," *New York Times*, July 9, 1998, section B, page 2, column 4, www.nytimes.com/1998/07/09/nyregion/public-lives-saving-images-of-dead-signs-on-old-walls.html.

SAVINGS, LOANS AND FUR VAULTS

141. Scripophily, "New York Bank History," www.scripophily.com/nybankhistoryg.htm.
142. *Advertising Age*, "Top Ten Slogans of the Century," adage.com/century/slogans.html.
143. Jennifer Bayot, "Stephen Baker, Ad Executive, Dies at 83," obituary, *New York Times*, September 24, 2004, www.nytimes.com/2004/09/24/obituaries/24baker.html.
144. Brooklyn Genealogy Information, "J.J. Friel," www.bklyn-genealogy-info.com/Town/Eastern/G.html.
145. *New York Times*, "Joseph John Friel," obituary, May 6, 1914, query.nytimes.com/gst/abstract.html?res=FB0713FC3C5E13738DDDAF0894DD405B848DF1D3.
146. *Fading Ad Blog*, "National Cold Storage—Brooklyn Bridge Park—Lawns Closed," April 4, 2010, http://www.fadingad.com/fadingadblog/?p=5959.
147. *Evening Citizen* [Ottawa, Ontario], "Proper Storage Protects Your Fur Coat Investment," April 11, 1944, 16, news.google.com/newspapers?id=LfYuAAAAIBAJ&sjid=9NsFAAAAIBAJ&dq=keeping%20your%20fur%20safe&pg=3012%2C1670749.

PAINT AND HARDWARE

148. George Carey-Simos, "Are Photographs Copies of the World?" University of Wales, Aberystwyth, www.aber.ac.uk/media/Students/gss99/gss9901.html.
149. George Carey-Simos, "Are Photographs Copies of the World?" University of Wales, Aberystwyth, www.gcsimos.com (updated website).
150. Robert Baptista, "Colorants Industry History," Colorant History, colorantshistory.org.
151. *Fading Ad Blog*, "Sunday's Feature Fade: The Despair of Port Arthur, Texas—Robert Baptista," March 9, 2008, www.fadingad.com/fadingadblog/?p=1053.
152. *Fading Ad Blog*, "Eaglo Paint Update from Robert Baptista," March 27, 2008, www.fadingad.com/fadingadblog/?p=1124.
153. Christian Warren, *Brush with Death: A Social History of Lead Poisoning* (Baltimore, MD: Johns Hopkins University Press, 2000), 23, books.google.com/books?id=bowkr3SNfLIC&pg=PA323&lpg=PA323&dq=%22Eaglo+Paint+and+Varnish+Corporation%22&source=bl&ots=ZNdF-aCNsk&sig=dLZ1-S0bez6beYoEvGpiv3S0SWY&hl=en&ei=rPIlTq-AC-aw0AGjiOjgCg&sa=X&oi=book_result&ct=result&resnum=5&ved=0CC4Q6AEwBA#v=onepage&q=%22Eaglo%20Paint%20and%20Varnish%20Corporation%22&f=false.
154. Harriet A.L. Standeven, *House Paints, 1900–1960: History and Use* (Hong Kong: Getty Publications, 2011), 93–94, books.google.com/books?id=1WviUh1u5UYC&pg=PA93&dq=%22Eaglo+Paint%22&hl=en&ei=3vAlTt__Jqio0AHYiMSvCg&sa=X&oi=book_result&ct=result&resnum=7&ved=0CGAQ6AEwBg#v=onepage&q=%22Eaglo%20Paint%22&f=false.
155. Jeremiah Moss, *Jeremiah's Vanishing New York*, "Tomb of Delphi," May 4, 2009, vanishingnewyork.blogspot.com/2009/05/tomb-of-delphi.html.

HORSE AND CARRIAGE

156. Joseph Berger, "Fading Memories," *New York Times*, November 5, 2005, query.nytimes.com/gst/fullpage.html?res=9B07E6DF143EF936A35752C1A9639C8B63&pagewanted=2.
157. Broadway Cares, www.broadwaycares.org/about_us.

158. Walsh, *Forgotten New York*, "Times Square Relic," www.forgotten-ny.com/ADS/Carriage/carriage.html.

159. Grutchfield, *New York City Signs: 14th to 42nd Street*, "Livery Stable," www.14to42.net/17street.html.

160. Nicholas Hirshon, "Fading Away on Brick Buildings throughout Queens, 'Ghost Signs' Advertise the Businesses and Product," *New York Daily News*, August 24, 2010, www.nydailynews.com/ny_local/queens/2010/08/24/2010-08-24_fading_away_on_brick_buildings_throughout_queens_ghost_signs_advertise_the_busin.html#ixzz1SheQkL2b.

161. Kennedy, "Saving Images of 'Dead Signs,'" *New York Times*.

FUEL, OIL, GAS AND COAL

162. "Coal Heating," *Model Railroader Magazine*, November 6, 2010, message thread, cs.trains.com/TRCCS/forums/t/181933.aspx#Diana%20Coal%20&%20Oil%20Co.

163. *Fading Ad Blog*, "Diana Coal & Oil Loses Her Top—East New York, Brooklyn," February 24, 2010, www.fadingad.com/fadingadblog/?p=5624.

164. Paragon Oil, "History," paragonoilco.com/?p=about.

165. von Wentzel Family Website, "Fuel Choices," www.vonwentzel.net/HVAC/FuelChoices/index.html.

166. See Fading Ad Wiki, fadingad.wikispaces.com/Fading+Ad+Vocabulary.

167. See Fading Ad Gallery Exhibitions Archive, www.fadingad.com/exhibit2.html.

MUSIC AND ENTERTAINMENT

168. Julian Seery Gude, *Julians.name*, "O.J. Gude and Me," www.blog.julians.name/2005/12/18/oj-gude-and-me.

169. Victor-Victrola, "Timeline of the Victor Phonograph Company," www.victor-victrola.com/Timeline.htm.

170. Wikipedia, "gramophone record," en.wikipedia.org/wiki/Gramophone_record.

171. The Digital Journalist, "M. Rappaport's Music Store, Jamaica, Queens, August 1997," October 2004, digitaljournalist.org/issue0410/disjpg04.html.

172. Dr. Michael Whitlatch, "Selwyn Theatre," Buena Vista University (Iowa), web.bvu.edu/faculty/whitlatch/42nd/selwyn.htm.

173. The New 42nd Street, "Our Theatres," www.new42.org/new42/new42_theaters.html.

174. Dunlap, "Old York," *New York Times*, www.nytimes.com/2000/12/10/nyregion/old-york-look-close-this-ever-new-town-you-will-see-traces-past-peeking-through.html.

175. Jay Shockley, "Apollo Theatre," Letter from the Landmarks Preservation Commission, June 28, 1983, www.neighborhoodpreservationcenter.org/db/bb_files/AT003.pdf.

176. Barry Singer, *Black and Blue: The Life and Lyrics of Andy Razaf* (New York: Schirmer, 1992), 142–43, cenhum.artsci.wustl.edu/files/cenhum/Monday_July_19_Afternoon_Session.pdf.

177. The NYC Chapter of the American Guild of Organists, "St. Paul's Community Church," www.nycago.org/Organs/NYC/html/StPaulCommunity.html.

178. Thaddeus Kochanny, "History: Heyday of the Player Piano," Automatic Musical Instrument Collectors' Association (Chicago Chapter), www.amica.org/Live/Instruments/Player_Pianos/Player_Piano_History.htm.

179. Wikipedia, "player piano," en.wikipedia.org/wiki/Player_piano.

180. Pianola, "Player Piano History and Development: Edwin Votey," www.pianola.com/pphist.htm.

181. Monrovia Sound Studio, www.doctorjazz.co.uk/index.html.

182. John Farrell, "Jean Lawrence Cook," Monrovia Sound Studio, March 2002, www.doctorjazz.co.uk/page11.html.

183. "Roll On, Imperial," *Time* magazine 41, no. 7, February 15, 1943, www.doctorjazz.co.uk/page11.html.

184. Kochanny, "History," www.amica.org/Live/Instruments/Player_Pianos/Player_Piano_History.html.

185. Player Pianos, "Duo Art Player Piano," www.playerpianos.com/2009/04/duo-art-player-piano.html; "Steinway Duo Art Player Piano, Unusual," youtu.be/5t5kX1l3FZw.

186. Prof. Alan Wallace, "Piano Roll, Rock 'n Roll," Monrovia Sound Studio, www.doctorjazz.co.uk/page11.html.

187. Mark Sommer, "The Day the Music Died," *Buffalo News*, January 3, 2009, www.buffalonews.com/incoming/article134934.ece.

188. New York State Department of State Division of Corporations, entity search, "Camera Mart," appext9.dos.state.ny.us/corp_public/CORPSEARCH.ENTITY_INFORMATION?p_nameid=436597&p_corpid=374326&p_entity_name=Camera%20Mart&p_name_type=%25&p_search_type=CONTAINS&p_srch_results_page=0.

189. Internet Movie Database, "Camera Mart," www.imdb.com/company/co0028623.

190. *Videography Magazine*, "Camera Mart," November 1980, www.experimentaltvcenter.org/history/pdf/AnconaGorewitz_74.pdf.

Hotels, Speakeasies and Saunas

191. Grutchfield quoting *New York Times*, February 21, 1916, 11.

192. Grutchfield quoting *New York Times*, July 4, 1924, 20.

193. Grutchfield, *New York City Signs: 14th to 42nd Street*, "Hotel Irvin," www.14to42.net/quik08.html.

194. Christopher Gray, "Streetscapes/The Henry Hudson Hotel, 353 West 57th Street; from Women's Clubhouse to WNET to $75 a night," *New York Times*, January 4, 1998, www.nytimes.com/1998/01/04/realestate/streetscapes-henry-hudson-hotel-353-west-57th-street-women-s-clubhouse-wnet-75.html.

195. Ibid.

196. Daniel B. Scheider, "Hell's Kitchen in the Raw," *New York Times*, August 27, 2000, www.nytimes.com/2000/08/27/nyregion/fyi-829021.html?pagewanted=print&src=pm.

197. James T. Young Family Genealogy Page, "Descendants of James T. 'Pop' Young," October 27, 2000) www.genealogy.com/users/y/o/u/James-T-Young/FILE/0006page.html.

198. Aviva Stampfer, "Mt. Morris Turkish Baths (Former): Popular Bathhouse and One of the Last in NYC, Founded in 1898," Place Matter, July 2010, www.placematters.net/node/1368.

199. Alan Feuer, "Mount Morris Journal; a Gay Bathhouse in Harlem? Hey, It's No Secret," *New York Times*, January 19, 2003, www.nytimes.com/2003/01/19/nyregion/mount-morris-journal-a-gay-bathhouse-in-harlem-hey-it-s-no-secret.html.

200. Ibid.

201. Stampfer, "Mt. Morris Turkish Baths."

202. See Kristin Loomis, "AIDS: The Numbers Game," *New York Magazine*, March 6, 1989, books.google.com/books?id=K-gCAAAAMBAJ&lpg=PA44&ots=laDh3zMoKJ&dq=Who%20was%20NYC%20health%20commissioner%20in%201988%20Stephen%20Joseph&pg=PA44#v=onepage&q&f=false

Rosario Dawson and Her Uncle Frank

203. Stay Close PFLAG, "Rosario Dawson and Uncle Frank," stayclose.org/campaign/celebrity.asp?id=9.

204. Stay Close PFLAG, "The Stay Close campaign," stayclose.org/campaign/default.asp.

Prostheses and Undertakers

205. "Pomeroy's Trusses," *The Proceedings of the Medical Society of the County of Kings* (1880), dspace.sunyconnect.suny.edu/bitstream/handle/1951/43289/proc1880.index.pdf?sequence=1.

206. "Pomeroy Truss Company," *The Pennsylvania Medical Journal* 9, no. 2 (1906), books.google.com/books?id=J6JEAAAAYAAJ&pg=PA153&lpg=PA153&dq=Pomeroy+Truss+Company+Brooklyn&source=bl&ots=Jl8D83QCKe&sig=VG6F3sw8lkB5a9jXG89vUsuFUs4&hl=en&ei=IkMkTurjKojV0QGZurjPAw&sa=X&oi=book_result&ct=result&resnum=1&ved=0CDgQ6AEwAA#v=onepage&q=Pomeroy%20Truss%20Company%20Brooklyn&f=false; "Pomeroy Truss Co – Livingston Street – March 1999" (July 19, 2011) Fading Ad Blog, http://www.fadingad.com/fadingadblog/?p=8699.

207. "Pomeroy Truss Co.," *Medical Directory of New York, New Jersey and Connecticut* (1910), www.archive.org/stream/medicaldirectory12medi/medicaldirectory12medi_djvu.txt.

208. Pomeroy Truss Company ad, National Institute of Health, archived, http://www.ncbi.nlm.nih.gov/pmc/articles/PMC2625107/pdf/jnma00778-0002.pdf

209. "Pomeroy ad," *Bulletin of the New York Academy of Medicine* (1941), http://www.ncbi.nlm.nih.gov/pmc/articles/PMC1933685/pdf/bullnyacadmed00568-0002.pdf.

210. "Arthur C. Pomeroy," Green-Wood Cemetery, Find a Grave, www.findagrave.com/cgi-bin/fg.cgi?page=gr&GRid=58706599.

211. *New York Times*, "Pomeroy," obituary, May 1, 1903, query.nytimes.com/gst/abstract.html?res=F50F14FC385D16738DDDA80894DD405B838CF1D3.

212. Ruth Bavetta, "Mother's Day, 1964," Good Reads, www.goodreads.com/story/show/24995-mother-s-day-1964.

213. Grutchfield, *New York City Signs: 14th to 42nd Street*, "G. Schoepfer (glass eyes) and Cottage Restaurant," www.14to42.net/32street6.html.

214. "Wm. W. Pecan," The Eastern District of Brooklyn, Brooklyn Genealogy, www.bklyn-genealogy-info.com/Town/Eastern/G.html.

215. "Wm. W. Pecan," Leading Manufacturers & Merchants: City of Brooklyn, Brooklyn Genealogy, www.bklyn-genealogy-info.com/Business/Progress/P/pecan473.html.

216. Evergreens Cemetery, "Stories," www.theevergreenscemetery.com/stories.

217. Evergreens Cemetery, "The Triangle Shirtwaist Fire," www.theevergreenscemetery.com/stories/shirtwaist-fire/the-triangle-shirtwaist-fire.

About the Author

Frank H. Jump is a New York City artist and educator. A native of Queens, New York, Jump has lived in Brooklyn with his husband, Vincenzo Aiosa, since 1989. Jump's first major photo exhibition ran at the New-York Historical Society from August to November 1998. After launching the Fading Ad Campaign website in February 1999, the debut of vintage hand-painted advertising on the Internet had a noticeable effect on popular culture, as evidenced by the subsequent proliferation of similar websites and blogs and the use of vintage advertising in television commercials, films and modern hand-painted ads. In the mid-2000s, Jump and Aiosa opened the Fading Ad Gallery in Brooklyn, where Jump's photography was on display for nearly two years, as well as having their curatorial debut with several shows featuring other HIV-positive visual artists and local Brooklyn artists of various media. Jump continues his documentation of these remnants of early advertising with the acclaimed *Fading Ad Blog*, a daily photo blog featuring images he and Aiosa have taken of ads worldwide, as well as the work of other fellow urban archaeologists. Jump teaches instructional technology, guitar, digital photography and other interdisciplinary studies at an elementary school in Flatbush, where he also resides.